Design Thinking

W0234395

Design Thinking is a set of strategic and creative processes and principles used in the planning and creation of products and solutions to human-centered design problems.

With design and innovation being two key driving principles, this series focuses on, but is not limited to, the following areas and topics:

- User Interface (UI) and User Experience (UX) Design

- Psychology of Design

- Human-Computer Interaction (HCI)

- Ergonomic Design

- Product Development and Management

- Virtual and Mixed Reality (VR/XR)

- User-Centered Built Environments and Smart Homes

- Accessibility, Sustainability and Environmental Design

- Learning and Instructional Design

- Strategy and best practices

This series publishes books aimed at designers, developers, storytellers and problem-solvers in industries to help them understand current developments and best practices at the cutting edge of creativity, to invent new paradigms and solutions, and challenge Creatives to push boundaries to design bigger and better than before.

More information about this series at https://link.springer.com/bookseries/15933.

The Art of Design Strategy

Tracing the Future of Design Innovation

Garkay Wong

Foreword by Andy Polaine, Design Leader and co-author of Service Design

Apress®

The Art of Design Strategy: Tracing the Future of Design Innovation

Garkay Wong
Berkeley, CA, USA

ISBN-13 (pbk): 979-8-8688-0551-6   ISBN-13 (electronic): 979-8-8688-0552-3

https://doi.org/10.1007/979-8-8688-0552-3

Managing Director, Apress Media LLC: Welmoed Spahr
Acquisitions Editor: James Robinson-Prior
Development Editor: James Markham
Coordinating Editor: Gryffin Winkler

Cover designed by eStudioCalamar

Distributed to the book trade worldwide by Apress Media, LLC, 1 New York Plaza, New York, NY 10004, U.S.A. Phone 1-800-SPRINGER, fax (201) 348-4505, e-mail orders-ny@springer-sbm.com, or visit www.springeronline.com. Apress Media, LLC is a California LLC and the sole member (owner) is Springer Science + Business Media Finance Inc (SSBM Finance Inc). SSBM Finance Inc is a **Delaware** corporation.

For information on translations, please e-mail booktranslations@springernature.com; for reprint, paperback, or audio rights, please e-mail bookpermissions@springernature.com.

Apress titles may be purchased in bulk for academic, corporate, or promotional use. eBook versions and licenses are also available for most titles. For more information, reference our Print and eBook Bulk Sales web page at http://www.apress.com/bulk-sales.

Any source code or other supplementary material referenced by the author in this book is available to readers on GitHub (https://github.com/Apress). For more detailed information, please visit https://www.apress.com/gp/services/source-code.

If disposing of this product, please recycle the paper

Dedicated to my mom.

Table of Contents

About the Author

Garkay Wong is a leading strategist and designer with extensive experience in the design services field. She currently works for one of the world's leading financial services companies as part of their design and strategy team.

Before her current role, she worked as an independent consultant guiding high-impact projects across diverse sectors—from Fortune 500 firms to public agencies and tech startups. She has a strong track record of merging strategy with practical innovation and has contributed articles on design and decision-making on platforms like Medium and the World Economic Forum.

About the Technical Reviewers

Eva Li is an accomplished product leader and serial entrepreneur with over a decade of expertise in innovation. As Head of Product at MTR Lab, she pioneered the venture studio with a proprietary methodology and drove smart mobility, EV, and living initiatives. Eva co-founded ImmiSearch, earning top national rankings in Canada and British Columbia's Business's 30 Under 30 recognition. Her work with STATSCONGO was featured in Forbes's 30 Under 30 healthcare category. A dedicated community builder, Eva is a sought-after speaker and mentor in product management and innovation.

Rupert Hetherton is a passionate Service Design leader with over 15 years innovating customer experiences across industries. He has delivered design projects in more than ten countries across Asia Pacific, working with some of the region's biggest companies to deliver customer delight and shareholder value. With a background in psychology, Rupert is passionate about learning and meeting the underlying needs of humans through transformed experiences. Expertise in design-driven innovation and transformation has made Rupert sought after as a leader, practitioner, and facilitator dedicated to advancing his craft.

Acknowledgments

I always thought writing a book would be a solitary endeavor, but this experience has taught me otherwise. Thank you to those who gave their time in contributing to the process. Because of all of you, I never felt alone.

First and foremost, I extend my heartfelt gratitude to Greg Solomon. You were one of the first to read my work when it was just a seedling of an idea. Your early feedback and encouragement motivated me to keep going. Ian Richardson and Martin Slaughter, thank you for contributing your expertise to develop these ideas in the early days. Your input on adapting structured decision-making to the field of design was key to shaping this work. I'm also extremely grateful to Andy Polaine, who made time between vacations and conferences to contribute a beautiful and inspiring foreword!

Thanks to Kevin Tong, Daniel Lee, Tracy Myers, Maria Edwards, and Neil Williams for providing feedback throughout and for agreeing to share your personal stories! The discussions we had were just the beginning. I could not be more grateful.

Special thanks to my technical reviewers, Rupert Hetherton and Eva Li, for contributing your knowledge and expertise. I have so much respect for you both. Your thoughtful builds and challenges to the material greatly strengthened the work.

To James Robinson-Prior and the Apress team—Jim Markham, Gryffin Winkler, Shonmirin P. A., and Deepa Tryphosa—thank you for believing in these ideas and taking a chance on this project. To editors Joel Mark Harris and Dr. Joseph Hurtgen—thank you for helping a designer insert her voice.

ACKNOWLEDGMENTS

I want to thank my mentor, Christine Tsang, who offered her support and guidance throughout the year. Your knack for knowing exactly when I needed a pep talk (or a reality check) made all the difference.

To my husband, Vincent, thank you for always encouraging me to pursue my wild ideas (and for being a good sport about sharing our stories!). I wouldn't want to do this with anyone else. Your support through all our life moments, big and small, means the absolute world to me.

Introduction

During the years of the design boom, designers seemed capable of transforming anything—even everyday objects like the shopping cart—into reimagined and better versions. Yet if we look around today, supermarket shopping carts remain unchanged.

This hints at a major problem—even innovative designs will fail if they do not align with business needs. For designs to be truly transformative, they must satisfy customer demands and organizational objectives.

Who the Book Is For

This book is for designers interested in design management and its implications, as well as those transitioning from design craft to management. Whether you're an independent contributor, a design lead managing a team, or just beginning your career, this book will provide you with the insights and tools needed to bridge the gap between design and business.

Who Will Benefit from This Book

- *Design Practitioners:* Professionals who want to understand the broader context of their work and how design strategy intersects with organizational goals

- *Professionals in Related Fields:* Executives and non-design professionals who want to learn how design can be applied strategically to foster an innovative mindset within their organizations

- *Academics and Researchers:* For those studying the practical applications of design thinking in the business world

What You Will Learn

This book introduces the TRACES framework, a suite of strategic tools to align design initiatives with organizational goals. To help you apply these tools effectively, the book is divided into four key parts, each exploring an important component of the framework.

Part I: "Do Things Better" focuses on optimizing current practices by aligning design aims with business outcomes. This part focuses on aligning on a strategic direction and identifying potential threats.

Part II: "Do Things at Scale" emphasizes scaling up capabilities through investments in people and technology. This part presents decision tools for selecting the solutions to support large-scale initiatives.

Part III: "Do Things Collaboratively" centers on building a design-led work culture. This part covers adaptive team structures and how to align them to business outcomes, how to communicate value to stakeholders, and how to cultivate a culture that values and integrates design thinking at every level.

Part IV: "Do Things Differently" talks about coping with unprecedented changes by leveraging design-led transformation. This part challenges us to think and work in different ways and leverage design to make a positive difference in the world around us.

What Else Should Readers Know?

We live in a time of great uncertainty. We are witnessing wars on multiple fronts, the rise of ethno-nationalism, challenges to democratic rule, and global warming. The tech landscape is changing faster than societies can cope and governments are struggling to contain the negative impacts of social media. It's important now more than ever for design to inform future business strategy and mitigate against these disruptions.

Design is the often-overlooked asset that can transform these problems into opportunities—not only to generate new ideas but to build real-world solutions that can help solve some of the most urgent problems we face today. The key difference of the design strategy approach outlined in this book is its focus on the interplay between organizational alignment and transformation. When we align our design efforts with business outcomes—whether it's increased profit or revenue, or the activities that contribute to those—the work of design can be transformative. Transformation is not just about innovating products and services but also the internal processes and cultures that define our organizations. Understanding how to use alignment to push for transformation will allow us not only to drive change within our companies but to also help shape the futures of the communities around us.

It's time to look beyond quarterly profits and take a more long-term view to build resilient organizations that can withstand uncertainty. Simply put—*design equals change*—and when aligned to business outcomes, it can be a powerful force for transformation and growth.

Focused innovation starts here.

Foreword

Throughout my 30 years in the design industry, predominantly in digital, design has always had to try to "prove its value." It is a discipline plagued with a reputation for being fuzzy, hand wavy, not grounded in solid numbers. This characterization has often put design in conflict with strategy folks, who are as fond of spreadsheets and PowerPoint as designers are of Sharpies and sticky notes.

Many designers have internalized and perpetuated this mischaracterization. These days, my professional focus is as a design leadership coach. I still hear plenty of confessions from design leads who feel they are not business savvy enough or that they find it difficult to "prove the ROI of design," even though they know from long experience that the work they do, spanning insight to strategy to implementation, has an impact across the entire business. The problem is this impact is not easily measurable or boiled down to a single number—the Holy Grail of C-Suite executives.

Yet the numbers in financial projections are just as much a fiction, hand wavy and fuzzy as a sketch of a future product or service. Arguably, the numbers are vaguer since at least the sketch is a tangible artifact that we can put in front of real people in context and test their responses.

Those projected numbers that appear so solid are illusionary, simply because nobody can predict the future. To make matters worse, an obsession with numerical metrics over people's behavior often leads to measuring what is easily measurable rather than what is important.

As I write this, Nike's dismal second quarter 2024 financial results were recently released. Nike lost around $25bn of market capitalization in one day ($70bn in nine months) and reached the lowest share price since 2018, a drop of 32% since the beginning of 2024.

Nike's poor performance is detailed in a scathing article by Brand Strategist and ex-Nike Senior Brand Director Massimo Giunco titled "Nike: An Epic Saga of Value Destruction." Giunco traced the misery back to 2020, when Nike's new CEO John Donahue decided Nike would become a direct-to-consumer company, wrecking its relationships with wholesale partners, and changing its marketing mode to be "data driven and digitally led."[1]

These decisions may have all made sense in a spreadsheet and, reportedly, McKinsey advised them on the strategy, no doubt promising millions in efficiency savings. Giunco reported how Nike's leadership were surprised by the "unexpected" consumer behavior that did not obey the projected numbers.

As Giunco put it, "Nike invested billions into something that was less effective but easier to be measured vs. something that was more effective but less easy to be measured."

Instead, consumers kept shopping where they were used to shopping, no longer saw Nike goods there, and switched to other brands. Something that anyone who understood people and their behavior could have foreseen.

Design, at its heart, is the practice of looking at something in the world and reimagining it. In a strategic role, design is extremely good at revealing behaviors and making ideas tangible, flipping the script on the perception of fuzziness. While corporate jargon and vague strategic claims, such as "data driven and digitally led," are fuzzy and hand wavy, designers will give you an artifact to show people and test.

In *The Art of Design Strategy*, Garkay Wong brings the best of both worlds together, demonstrating how design strategy is as grounded in pattern recognition, research, analysis, and expertise as any projection

---

[1] https://www.linkedin.com/pulse/nike-epic-saga-value-destruction-massimo-giunco-11plf/.

or financial model. Garkay provides the materials you need to develop a strategic direction—through the TRACES framework, workshop structures, canvases, and matrices—and the means to align the organization around it.

In this alignment, many organizations fail in their transformations but this is also where design's ability to make the intangible tangible can be most potent. Exceptionally well-designed products and services often appear inevitable, as if they could have only ever been that way, but it can take many iterations to get to that point. Design often appears subjective because the many decisions leading to the final outcome are invisible. This works well for the end user but makes it an enigma for stakeholders, especially in large organizations.

The decision tools in this book can help provide a clear traceability of how decisions were made, adding transparency and accountability to the design process. It provides a framework for justifying our design choices more rigorously, allowing us to more easily demonstrate that elusive value at the other end.

I wish you and all and the organizations you work for great success.

Andy Polaine, PhD
Offenburg, August 2024

Why This Book Was Written

A design legend I knew in the banking industry was laid off after a particularly challenging stint as a senior executive. Reflecting on our meeting less than a year earlier, all the signs were there. What started as a casual meeting led to a deeper discussion about the ongoing struggle for design leadership to justify investments into their initiatives in a way that resonates with C-suite executives.

In our chat, I questioned my approach, wondering if I truly understood how to justify design to executives looking through the lens of P&L statements. As we said our goodbyes, he made a cryptic comment suggesting we revisit our conversation later in the year with a telling remark, "If I'm still here by then."

It wasn't long before I understood why. Despite his visionary status, he faced challenges within the corporate hierarchy, confined by constraints and budgets set without his input. His frustration wasn't with the corporate standards, per se, but in finding effective ways to defend and expand his design vision within those limits. Our conversation was less a challenge to my design choices and more a reflection of his struggle to champion his team in a restrictive and unyielding environment.

This experience is not isolated. In the past few years, we've seen similar departures of high-profile design leaders across industries, from tech to retail to healthcare. This trend raises a critical question: *Why is design often the first on the chopping block during cost-cutting?*

At the time of writing, many seasoned design leaders are grappling with this question. Greg Petroff, an experienced design leader who has held senior roles at GE, Google, and ServiceNow, echoed this sentiment in Robert Fabricant's article about design leaders: "As leaders, we need to learn how to be really awesome stewards with resources. We need to defend the investment in design with total clarity. That part is new."[2]

Having had similar struggles as the banking executive, the imperative to clearly defend design investments resonated with me. I realized a crucial bridge is needed at the intersection of design and business. My friend in the banking sector was a design leader and a visionary in every right, equipped with creative prowess and an MBA. Yet, he grappled with the challenge of justifying not only his team's value in a way that resonates with C-suite executives, but also his own. His struggle is a common one in the design field. Even highly qualified design leaders struggle to justify the value of design in a corporate environment.

Since I began writing this book, I've interacted with and interviewed designers at various career stages, including mid-level professionals and senior design leaders. This experience has been enriched by research and consultations with non-design experts from different industries, focusing on the adaptation of their tools and frameworks for the design field. These conversations helped shape the methods and approaches featured in this book to connect design strategies back to business objectives.

How to Use This Book

What is the business value of user delight when customers interact with a well-designed product? Conversely, what is the cost to a company when customers experience frustration during critical moments?

---

[2] Fabricant, Robert, "The Big Design Freak-Out: A Generation of Design Leaders Grapple with Their Future," Fast Company, 15 Feb. 2024, https://www.fastcompany.com/91027996/the-big-design-freak-out-a-generation-of-design-leaders-grapple-with-their-future.

Peter Drucker, a key figure in developing modern management practices, said, *"If you can't measure it, you can't improve it."* Drucker's quote will likely resonate with executives whose focus is on measurable goals like growth and efficiency. Data and reporting are heavily emphasized because numbers make it easier to make informed decisions and track progress toward achieving goals. Companies tend to over-index on what is easy to measure, and while traditional metrics can be useful, they often do not tell the whole story of design's impact on the customer experience. What unfortunately happens is that because these considerations are difficult to quantify, they are simply overlooked. Unless design initiatives can be clearly linked to driving these priorities, they are unlikely to garner interest from executives, so having the ability to connect design efforts to these priorities is essential.

As designers, we intuitively know that user satisfaction and customer loyalty are key drivers of profitability. However, designers must communicate the value of design in terms executives can understand. For instance, if a company is planning aggressive pricing strategies that prioritize short-term profits at the expense of design quality and service, it's important to articulate the risks. Strategies focused on making quick cash grabs can tarnish a brand's reputation and lead customers to seek alternatives, especially when they feel they're not getting their money's worth. This not only has a direct impact on the bottom line but can potentially undermine investor confidence. Similarly, cost-cutting measures that lead to poorly designed product interfaces can escalate customer service costs and, along with user dissatisfaction, permanently drive customers away.

We live in an age of transparency where customers can share negative reviews of any service or app. One bad experience can expose the limitations of an organization's marketing and PR teams in mitigating these issues. Take, for example, Youtuber Marques Brownlee (widely recognized by his YouTube handle @MKBHD) who reviewed a product called the Humane AI Pin for his almost 20 million subscribers, calling it the worst product he'd ever seen. While Marques Brownlee was not alone in his critique of the AI Pin, he is so influential in the tech space his review almost certainly put the nail in the coffin for the product and the company itself. Humane was hoping to sell at least 100,000 units the first year but only sold about 10,000 with over 1,000 pre-orders canceled after the reviews were posted online. The launch of the AI Pin was a textbook example of what not to do.

However, Humane is not alone in botched launches. Design teams are often brought into the conversation after the damage has been done, left with the dual challenge of urgent fixes and the imperative to not only meet but exceed customer expectations in a short time frame. Not only does it add to cost but it puts significant pressure on designers to resolve issues that could have been avoided with their earlier strategic involvement.

As design leaders, it's our responsibility to elevate the design agenda to a strategic level within our organizations. Doing so requires the careful selection of tools that foster design and innovation and ensure the value of design is clearly understood by the rest of the business. By demonstrating the impact of design and how it can be leveraged to drive business success, we can position design as a strategic asset deeply embedded in the core values and overall mission of the companies we work for.

Aligning Design with Business Strategy

Design and business leaders share a common goal: create exceptional products and services that drive the long-term financial sustainability of businesses. With this common goal in mind, the question becomes: "How can design and business teams better align around strategies to deliver exceptional customer experiences?"

The culmination of my thoughts on these efforts is the TRACES framework, a suite of tools I've designed to address the key challenges around aligning design and business goals. In the opening chapters, the framework guides you to establish an initial link between these shared objectives (Chapter 2). TRACES then facilitates the identification of external risks that may trigger further strategic adjustment (Chapter 3), along with mitigation planning and targeted budget allocation (Chapter 4). This phase concentrates on maintenance, ensuring the optimization of current operations.

As we move through the process, you might find it necessary to realign or pivot your growth plans (Chapter 6). This discovery could lead to thoughtful consideration of strategic investments in your teams, technology, or even your entire business model.

The later chapters present tools to support one of three growth pathways: enhancement via technologies (Chapter 5), adaptation via structure and teams (Chapters 8 and 9), and full-scale transformation (Chapter 11), depending on the organization's growth strategy and situational needs.

These exercises are modular and adaptable, allowing you to use them as you see fit. You can follow the recommended sequence or pick the tools that make sense, depending on where you are in your design process and what decision(s) need to be made.

Aligning Design Strategy with Business Outcomes

How do we bridge the gap between our creative processes and the business-focused language of our executive counterparts? The answer lies in aligning our efforts with business outcomes.

Tracing success directly to design outcomes is challenging but not impossible. Each chapter in this book begins with a story that highlights the challenges and successes of strategic design integration. It then introduces a strategic alignment tool aimed at bridging design and business objectives. A workshop section details how to apply these concepts practically and provides guidance on which stakeholders should attend. At the conclusion of each chapter, we provide key takeaways to facilitate the translation of design values into common business terminology.

A Foundational Framework

Design is not often thought of as a strategic function, but there is a growing need for designers to have access to their own business tools, frameworks, and language to effectively communicate the value of design to senior executives. Designers may be hesitant to step out of their traditional roles but much of the value of design comes from leveraging it to drive business outcomes. The TRACES framework is a response to these emerging needs, equipping designers with what they need to bridge that gap.

Like any method, the TRACES framework has its limitations and trade-offs. I invite readers to engage critically with the framework and view it as a part of an ongoing dialogue in Strategic Design rather than a definitive answer.

The past two decades have seen the field of design transform significantly, driven by the ubiquity of smartphones and ecommerce. During this time, the immediate focus was to explore and identify opportunities with new modes of interaction on mobile and the Web. It makes perfect sense, therefore, that many of the traditional design methods and tools we use today emphasize discovery and ideation. Since then, design has matured. What's often missing from the design toolkit are tools that can help us assess and prepare the organization for the broader strategic impact of design change. We need tools that can help not only in choosing which ideas to pursue but also give us a good understanding of how well-aligned our design efforts are to the company's strategic goals and how prepared our organization is to implement said changes. Armed with this knowledge, we can better justify the investments needed to deliver meaningful outcomes.

A great creative vision need not conflict with business strategy. Instead, aligning our efforts around common goals ensures that we get the best outcomes from our people, our processes, and our technology. We're not limiting our creativity as designers when we design with business constraints in mind. Quite the opposite—in the eyes of the organization, we are amplifying our impact. If this divide is acknowledged, we can align ourselves to focus on solutions instead of what sets us apart.

Reframing Conversations Around the "Value of Design"

The frameworks and tools we adopt reflect what we claim to value. Placing design at the heart of organizational strategy is a deliberate choice. The promise of design—its capacity to solve problems, drive change, and foster innovation—transforms into a strategic advantage only when organizations choose to integrate design into their core business functions. To realize the benefits, design strategy must be supported by robust tools that provide clear and defensible methods for evaluating options, mitigating risks, and allocating resources.

The frameworks and tools I introduce in this book aim to ensure that design efforts align with business goals and address the strategic challenges faced by design and business leaders. By broadening the definition of value to include aspects of design that are harder to measure—yet are essential for delivering value to customers—we aim to position the design function as a key partner in driving business success. I believe these tools will enable design leaders to communicate design's value effectively and help organizations leverage its full potential.

So, let's dive in and get started.

CHAPTER 1

The Rise of Design Strategy

Today, design is in a state of flux. Robert Fabricant's article "The Big Design Freak-Out: Generation of Design Leaders Grapple with Their Future" hit a nerve among designers—and rightly so. Given major layoffs at IDEO and IBM and the elimination of design leadership roles at major corporations, it's not surprising that designers everywhere are worried about their future. Over the years, I've seen the role of design in organizations grow, yet the inability to connect design efforts directly to business outcomes often places the value of design under scrutiny.

In this chapter, you will learn the following:

- How the perception of design in organizations has evolved

- The need to create a link between design operations and overarching business strategies

- How new frameworks, tools, and methodologies can help bridge the gap between design and organizational strategy

© Garkay Wong 2025
G. Wong, *The Art of Design Strategy*, Design Thinking,
https://doi.org/10.1007/979-8-8688-0552-3_1

The Current State of Design

A friend of mine used to work at Grab in its early days, when it was establishing itself as Southeast Asia's largest ride-hailing app. He once shared with me that one of the most contentious issues at his company was around the app's home screen. Entire departments battled over its design layout. Many people might wonder what the big deal is. It's this— when you change the home screen, you're not just rearranging arbitrary design elements, you're proposing to alter backend processes and business dynamics—determining which partnerships and service categories—such as food delivery vs. ride-hailing—receive visibility and how these changes affect the teams involved in each area.

An app's redesign impacts each team differently. Even seemingly minor tweaks like adding a button to make it easier to cancel rides can have direct implications on the bottom line. These arguments can get quite heated and, of course, the stakeholders are all going to have opinions on what they think is best. Throughout my career, I've witnessed designers get stuck in the middle of these arguments. But without decision-making power, we often get dragged into disagreements that aren't about the design itself, but rather the strategy behind it. That's why we need to arm ourselves with a deep understanding of the outcomes our stakeholders are trying to achieve and of the strategic goals and frameworks that guide their decision-making. This knowledge allows us to be better partners, helping stakeholders to understand the potential benefits, risks, and trade-offs of our design decisions.

From Cost Center to Value Creator: The Evolution of Design's Role

Many of us enter this field driven by a genuine love for design. I'm no different. As a kid, I struggled to get my thoughts out in words. The words would tumble out of my mouth before my brain could process what I was saying. Eventually, I realized I could put my ideas on paper. I could communicate so much with a sketch *and* it was an easier way for me to connect with people than speaking. Design has the power to help us express our ideas visually. It allows us to solve problems, think creatively, and make a meaningful difference in the lives of users—all while seeing our ideas come to life! These are the qualities that inspire so many of us to join the profession. But as we advance in our careers, many of us realize that climbing the career ladder requires more than that. Rather than just doing the hands-on design work, we need to learn how to manage, lead, and make strategic decisions. Balancing our passion for hands-on design with the demands of leadership allows us to grow professionally and create greater value for the people and teams we work with and design for.

The other night, I was watching the movie *Top Gun: Maverick* with my husband. Tom Cruise's character Pete "Maverick" Mitchell spent over 30 years in the US Navy and was awarded numerous combat decorations. Yet to the disappointment of his seniors, he refuses to conform to the traditional Navy career path. At one point, his commanding officer tells him, "You should be at least a two-star admiral by now, if not a senator. Yet here you are: Captain." Maverick spent his career perfecting his command of the skies, becoming one of the US Navy's best pilots. Now, he finds himself tasked with directing and coaching the next generation of pilots. Instead of flying in the blue skies overhead, he's in the trenches navigating bureaucracy, and handling the strategic, logistical, and political complexities of leadership. As I watched the movie, I thought, "The dude loves to fly—just let him fly!"

Designers have a similar love for their craft. We love to design! But as we climb the career ladder, we must take on new roles and responsibilities. Managing teams, aligning with stakeholders, and dealing with organizational politics can feel far removed from the hands-on design work that drew us to the field. The higher we go, the more we need to balance our passion for design with leadership, communication, and strategic thinking skills. But many designers might say, "Hang on, I didn't sign up for that!"

It's true that our design education doesn't prepare us for this transition, but without developing business skills beyond our core competencies and preparing for leadership roles, we can't achieve the larger aim of elevating design within our organizations. Where would Apple be without Jony Ive and his iconic designs for the iPhone or the MacBook or Microsoft without Bill Buxton and his approach to design and user experience? Without designers willing to step up into leadership positions within the organization, design will always be relegated to a secondary role.

There is often a misconception that design activities are not positive contributors to revenue generation but rather incur costs that need to be minimized. It's no surprise that when financial challenges arise, design budgets are among the first to face cuts. The focus is on saving costs rather than investing in enhancing user experiences or driving innovation. In such settings, design often scrambles to react to changing business needs instead of proactively shaping them.

A CEO might initially make decisions that prioritize short-term gains but this can hurt their user base over time. If this continues, customers will switch their allegiance to competitors. Yet companies still behave as if customers can't easily turn to a competitor if their needs aren't met. This outdated mindset fails to recognize the empowered consumers of today. In the digital age, customers can quickly compare options and make informed choices.

Oftentimes, executives fail to see this and regard design as an optional nice-to-have, a corner that can be cut as long as the end product is delivered. Addressing this gap requires going beyond being just a supporting function or yet another siloed-off innovation lab. We need to bring design back into the boardroom and elevate it to a strategic level. This will ensure that design is deeply integrated into the core strategy, and help us to influence key decisions that shape the company's direction. Unless we do this, design will always be seen as an optional cost center rather than as a critical component that drives revenue growth.

Design can unlock significant value when channeled to problem-solve, manage change, and differentiate from competitors. Zoom out far enough and we see design as a powerful driver of sustainable growth and innovation. By ensuring the organization is not merely chasing short-term profits, we can set up a resilient, forward-thinking strategy. Investing in design is not just about profit and differentiation; it is also about resilience and the ability to deal with change.

As the pace of disruption accelerates and rapid change becomes the norm, products that are relevant today could be meaningless tomorrow. Businesses must continuously innovate to stay ahead of the curve. However, before we can unlock large-scale innovation and chart a course, we have to understand our current state. Design maturity at the organizational level plays a key role in this process.

The History of Design

Alan Cooper released the first edition of his pioneering book *About Face* in the early days of interaction design. At the time, the graphic interface design was primarily handled by software developers[1] and design's prominence within organizations was still emerging from the bottom up. Cooper and a small cohort of developers had what was then considered a radical idea: What if we design technology to suit user needs? This sounds like common sense now, but until his manifesto, this line of thinking was rare. It was the shot across the bow that challenged practitioners to rethink their approach and create software users would love.[2]

Before Cooper's idea of user-centric design, only a small handful of forward-thinking companies like Yahoo, Microsoft, and Apple developed in-house design capability, bringing in the likes of Susan Kare, a graphic designer who created many of the systems icons we are familiar with today. Apple recognized the importance of design early, even if it played

---

[1] Cooper, Alan, About Face: The Essentials of Interaction Design, August 1995, page x of the Foreword.

[2] Cooper, About Face, page x of the Foreword.

a supporting role at first. We see the fingerprints of these early in-house design teams in early versions of Microsoft Windows, such as 1.0 and 2.0 featuring basic graphic user interfaces.[3]

The 2000s marked a turning point as design and technology converged. To paraphrase Steve Jobs on the launch of the iPhone in 2007, it "changed everything." Google's clean, simple user interface transformed search, Apple's iPhone redefined how people access the Internet and Amazon changed the way we shop. Today, most of us can't go a few hours without Googling something. I can look up reviews on my iPhone to find highly rated restaurants for dinner and order just about anything online knowing it will be delivered to my doorstep within a day or two. This era changed the game for the field of design and designers, demonstrating how innovative designs can make a difference in everyone's lives.

Companies saw the difference design made and rushed to meet these expectations. This drove a dramatic shift in product development. As design started to play a more central role in shaping the user experience, the back and forth working with external agencies became too slow and inefficient. Many companies saw the value of integrating design into their core product discussions and began to hire and expand their in-house teams. In some cases, large corporations like Capital One acquired design agencies like Adaptive Path to bring this coveted expertise in-house.[4] More and more companies began building in-house teams, and as these teams grew, so did the need for better processes and workflows to manage these teams effectively. This led to the emergence of Design Operations (or DesignOps), which streamlined workflows and established standardized

---

[3] Microsoft Windows, Wikipedia, The Free Encyclopedia, Wikimedia Foundation, 1 June 2024, en.wikipedia.org/wiki/Microsoft_Windows. Accessed 2 June 2024.

[4] Ha, Anthony, "Design Firm Adaptive Path Acquired by Capital One," TechCrunch, 2 Oct. 2014, https://techcrunch.com/2014/10/02/adaptive-path-acquired-by-capital-one/.

processes to improve the efficiency of these teams. Figure 1-1 summarizes the evolution of design, leading to our current moment at the cusp of the next big shift in design.

The Five Epochs in the Evolution of Digital Product Design

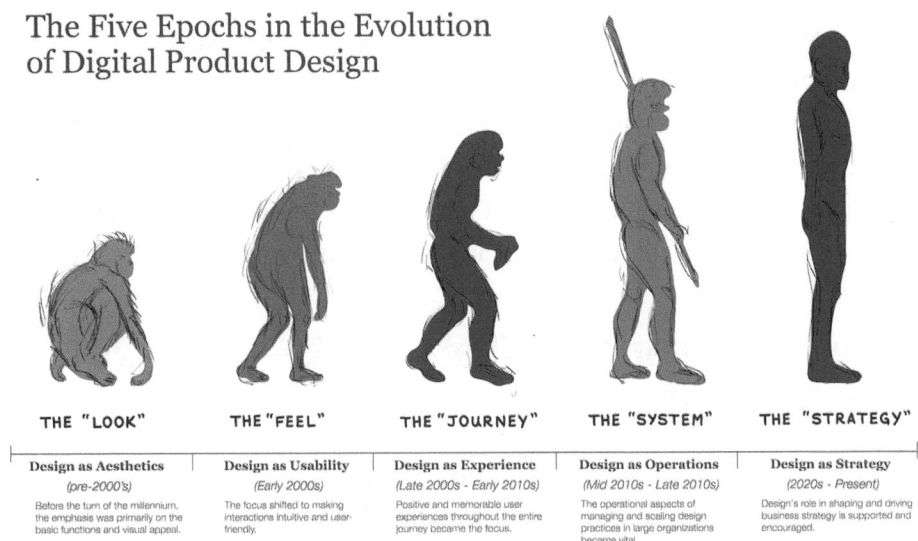

THE "LOOK"	THE "FEEL"	THE "JOURNEY"	THE "SYSTEM"	THE "STRATEGY"
Design as Aesthetics	**Design as Usability**	**Design as Experience**	**Design as Operations**	**Design as Strategy**
(pre-2000's)	*(Early 2000s)*	*(Late 2000s - Early 2010s)*	*(Mid 2010s - Late 2010s)*	*(2020s - Present)*
Before the turn of the millennium, the emphasis was primarily on the basic functions and visual appeal.	The focus shifted to making interactions intuitive and user-friendly.	Positive and memorable user experiences throughout the entire journey became the focus.	The operational aspects of managing and scaling design practices in large organizations became vital.	Design's role in shaping and driving business strategy is supported and encouraged.

Figure 1-1. *How the role of design within organizations evolved over time*

Design as Aesthetics (Pre-2000s) "The Look"

Under Steve Jobs' vision and leadership, Apple was one of the rare companies that made design a core part of their identity. Design wasn't just an afterthought for Jobs—he was the architect of emphasizing design first, including professional looking fonts, rounded edges, and high-quality materials. Other companies may have acknowledged design, but they saw it as little more than a way to make products look good. If design was involved, it was after all the key technology and business decisions had already been made. Apple, in contrast, understood that design could shape the entire user experience.

Design as Usability (Early 2000s) "The Feel"

With increasingly complex web applications and the intrusive prevalence of pop-ups, the importance of usability became more prominent in the early 2000s. Usability, which refers to the ease with which a user can interact with a product or system to achieve their goals effectively, efficiently, and satisfactorily, became a critical focus. Businesses realized that users needed to navigate websites smoothly to complete desired actions, whether it was making a purchase or accessing information. Design began to pivot toward creating intuitive, user-friendly interfaces, making usability a primary consideration.

Design as Experience (Late 2000s—Early 2010s) "The Journey"

Triggered by the smartphone revolution and proliferation of apps, design emphasis shifted from usability to crafting comprehensive user experiences. Experience refers to the overall perception and response a person has when interacting with a product, service, or system, including all aspects of the interaction, such as usability, accessibility, performance, design, and emotional reactions. The entire user journey, encompassing every touchpoint and emotion, became paramount. This era marked the rise of holistic user experience (UX) design, which considered everything from user interaction to emotional resonance. My husband can shout "Open Source!" "configurability!" and "Linux!" until he's blue in the face, but I'll always appreciate the seamless experience of Apple products.

Design as Operations (Mid-2010s—Late 2010s) "The System"

Digital products became integral to business ecosystems in the early to late 2010s. As the complexities of managing design grew, DesignOps emerged as a critical function. DesignOps focuses on the operational aspects of design, optimizing and streamlining design processes to improve efficiency, collaboration, consistency, and overall effectiveness. DesignOps ensures that design workflows, tools, and resources are managed effectively, creating a scalable and sustainable environment for design. Design systems were introduced to address the challenge of fragmented efforts and inconsistent interfaces. They provided reusable design components and guidelines, ensuring interface consistency, scalability, and user-friendliness, thus anchoring design as a unified endeavor to achieve broader business objectives.

Design as Strategy (2020s) "The Strategy"

As we navigate this next decade, the rapid acceleration of technological change highlights the urgency of recognizing design as a core strategic pillar. Companies at the forefront understand the importance of integrating design into their business strategy, a plan of action designed to achieve long-term business goals and competitive advantage. They understand the crucial role design plays in transformation, how it can help businesses pivot to changing customer preferences and adapt to uncertain situations in a fast-changing market. However, not all organizations have fully embraced this shift. For many—even those who understand the promise of design—the challenge remains in bridging the tactical practices of design with the strategic imperatives of the business, which involves making decisions on resource allocation, market positioning, product development, and operations management to drive long-term success.

Assessing Design Capability

I spoke with a transformation manager who relies heavily on data and reporting who was surprised that designers don't typically produce extensive reports and assessments. In her role, assessments are indispensable for tracking the progress of any initiative. As she aptly put it, "Otherwise, how would you demonstrate the change?" Utilizing reports and assessments is integral to her function, enabling her to secure the budget and justify investments effectively.

So, before diving into strategy and innovation, let's assess and reflect on our own level of design capability. By understanding our current capabilities and how they measure up, we can make sure that each action we take contributes to the change we seek.

The Design Capability Model, shown in Figure 1-2, is a framework for evaluating and understanding a company's design capabilities and identifying potential areas for improvement. While it doesn't directly measure organizational *performance*, it provides a view of an organization's design *capability* across six distinct categories:

- Design as Aesthetics

- Design as Usability

- Design as Experience

- Design as Operations

- Design as Strategy

- Design as a Force for Good

The categories capture the different ways that design can serve a business and provides a holistic view of what a well-rounded design function can look like.

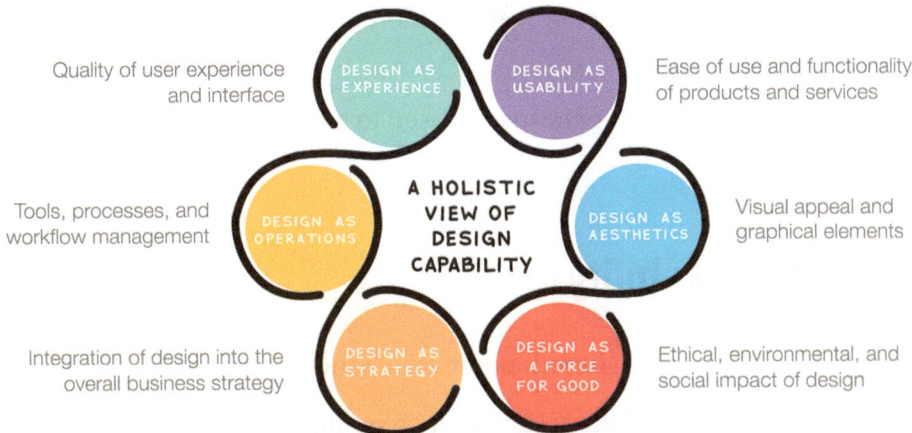

Figure 1-2. *Design capability model*

Each category has five related statements for individual or organizational reflection. The statements are designed to assess your level of confidence in achieving design excellence in that area.

Design as Aesthetics

- Visual appeal and graphical elements of design

- *Improvement Focus:* How well are visual elements organized to engage users and reduce cognitive load?

Statements for Reflection:

- Color, type, and images are used effectively to engage users

- Dense content is grouped into chunks to reduce cognitive load

- Consistent visual elements and terms are maintained throughout the design

- Accessibility for people with different abilities is considered

- Familiar design patterns are used to solve common UI issues

Design as Usability

- Ease of use and functionality of products and services

- *Improvement Focus:* How well do we address core usability issues like navigation, content hierarchy, and feedback?

Statements for Reflection:

- Navigation is clear and consistent with a complete flow

- Content is structured with a clear hierarchy for user prioritization

- Timely and informative feedback is provided for user actions

- The design adapts seamlessly to different devices and screen sizes

- Users can customize their experiences based on their preferences

Design as Experience

- Quality of user experience and interface

- *Improvement Focus:* How well do we foster positive, engaging user journeys?

Statements for Reflection:

- Frustration is minimized by ensuring users can complete tasks easily

- Clear guidance used throughout the user journey to reduce confusion

- Clear steps outlined to boost satisfaction and achieve user goals

- Interactive elements for exploration strengthen engagement

- Designs create delight by exceeding user expectations

Design as Operations

- Tools, processes, and workflow management in design

- *Improvement Focus:* How well do we streamline design operations by optimizing tools, processes, and systems?

Statements for Reflection:

- Design teams have the necessary tools to meet project demands

- Standardized design processes reduce time spent on repetitive tasks

- Feedback loops refine and adapt processes to changing needs

- Design systems offer unified guidelines, components, and assets

- New hires are onboarded to cover culture, tools, and processes

Design as Strategy

- Strategic integration of design into overall business objectives

- *Improvement Focus:* How well do design initiatives support strategic goals and drive meaningful business outcomes?

Statements for Reflection:

- Design initiatives are aligned with the strategic goals of the organization

- Plans are in place to address potential threats to the strategy

- Strategic decisions consider all available options and criteria

- Resources are allocated to design areas that drive business outcomes

- The impact of design is recognized and valued within the organization

Design as a Force for Good

- Ethical, environmental, and social impact of design

- *Improvement Focus:* How well do design initiatives create shared value and address global challenges?

Statements for Reflection:

- Design helps redesign business models and mindsets for sustainability

- Design initiatives balance business goals with global imperatives

- Design efforts are driven by a shared commitment to improving lives

- Partnerships are built with companies and communities for greater impact

- The business creates economic value while addressing societal challenges

Not only does this model highlight our current position, it also offers a roadmap for improvement. It provides benchmarks against which we can measure our capabilities and track our progress. More importantly, it offers opportunities for introspection, allowing us to recognize our strengths and areas where growth is needed.

Understanding the Assessment

Before we go deeper into the design assessment, it's important to understand the underlying logic. Capability assessments help companies identify their strengths and weaknesses. This isn't just about understanding where you stand. By assessing current capabilities, companies can pinpoint areas needing improvement, and allocate resources accordingly.

- Holistic View: Mapping our design capability scores on a radar chart helps us to visualize design capabilities as a whole, while simultaneously revealing strengths and weaknesses across different design competencies.

- Identifying Gaps: Visual representation makes it easier to identify where additional resources or focus may be required and allow companies to plan targeted development initiatives.

- Benchmarking: Compare a company's design capabilities relative to competitors or industry standards. By identifying areas where they might be underperforming, teams can prioritize improvement efforts effectively.

The Design Capability Assessment (Figure 1-3) provides a way to assess how confident individuals or organizations are in their ability to deliver across the six Design Capability levels. This approach helps companies and design leaders pinpoint areas that need improvement and identify opportunities to build design capability.

For each of the six categories of design capability—Design as Aesthetics, Design as Usability, Design as Experience, Design as Operations, Design as Strategy, and Design as a Force for Good—you will be asked to rate your organization's confidence in delivering results in that area.

Multiple individuals, whether within the design function or across related functions, should take this assessment. The scores should be averaged across all assessments to obtain a broad view of capability. This solicitation approach bolsters the defensibility of the assessment results. The facilitator will also gain insight into any areas of particularly strong disagreement regarding capability, which may suggest a disconnect that needs to be addressed.

Design Capability Assessment

Instructions:
1. Read on each statement.
2. Rate your organization on a scale of 1 (Not Confident) to 5 (Extremely Confident) based on your current situation.
3. Add up the scores for each category and divide by 5 to get the average score.
4. Map your confidence level onto a radar chart.

(1) - Not Confident   **(2)** - Slightly Confident   **(3)** - Moderately Confident   **(4)** - Very Confident   **(5)** - Extremely Confident

1 Design as Aesthetics

Rate your confidence level

	1	2	3	4	5
1. Color, type and images are used effectively to engage users	☐	☐	☐	☐	☐
2. Dense content is grouped in chunks to reduce cognitive load	☐	☐	☐	☐	☐
3. Consistent visual elements and terms are maintained throughout	☐	☐	☐	☐	☐
4. Accessibility for people with different abilities are considered	☐	☐	☐	☐	☐
5. Familiar design patterns are used to solve common UI issues	☐	☐	☐	☐	☐

Example of Practice

Average Score: ___ / 5.00

2 Design as Usability

Rate your confidence level

	1	2	3	4	5
1. Navigation is clear and consistent with complete flows	☐	☐	☐	☐	☐
2. Content is structured with a clear hierarchy for user prioritization	☐	☐	☐	☐	☐
3. Timely and informative feedback is provided for user actions	☐	☐	☐	☐	☐
4. Design adapts seamlessly to different devices and screen sizes	☐	☐	☐	☐	☐
5. Users can customize their experiences based on their preferences	☐	☐	☐	☐	☐

Example of Practice

Average Score: ___ / 5.00

3 Design as Experience

Rate your confidence level

	1	2	3	4	5
1. Frustration is minimized by ensuring users can complete tasks easily	☐	☐	☐	☐	☐
2. Clear guidance used throughout the user journey to reduce confusion	☐	☐	☐	☐	☐
3. Clear steps are outlined to boost satisfaction and achieve user goals	☐	☐	☐	☐	☐
4. Interactive elements for exploration strengthen engagement	☐	☐	☐	☐	☐
5. Designs aim to create delight by exceeding user expectations	☐	☐	☐	☐	☐

Example of Practice

Average Score: ___ / 5.00

4 Design as Operations

Rate your confidence level

	1	2	3	4	5
1. Design teams have the necessary tools to meet project demands	☐	☐	☐	☐	☐
2. Standardized processes help reduce time on repetitive tasks	☐	☐	☐	☐	☐
3. Feedback loops help to refine / adapt processes to changing needs	☐	☐	☐	☐	☐
4. Design systems offer unified guidelines, components and assets	☐	☐	☐	☐	☐
5. New hires are onboarded to cover culture, tools, and processes	☐	☐	☐	☐	☐

Example of Practice

Average Score: ___ / 5.00

5 Design as Strategy

Rate your confidence level

	1	2	3	4	5
1. Design initiatives are aligned to the strategic goals of the organization	☐	☐	☐	☐	☐
2. Plans are in place to address any potential threats to the strategy	☐	☐	☐	☐	☐
3. Strategic decisions have considered all available options and criteria	☐	☐	☐	☐	☐
4. Resources are allocated to design areas that drive business outcomes	☐	☐	☐	☐	☐
5. The impact of design is recognized and valued within the organization	☐	☐	☐	☐	☐

Example of Practice

Average Score: ___ / 5.00

6 Design as Force for Good

Rate your confidence level

	1	2	3	4	5
1. Design helps redesign business models and mindsets for sustainability	☐	☐	☐	☐	☐
2. Design initiatives align with business goals and global imperatives	☐	☐	☐	☐	☐
3. Design efforts are driven by a shared commitment to improving lives	☐	☐	☐	☐	☐
4. Partnerships are built with companies and communities for greater impact	☐	☐	☐	☐	☐
5. Business creates economic value while addressing societal challenges	☐	☐	☐	☐	☐

Example of Practice

Average Score: ___ / 5.00

Figure 1-3. *Design capability assessment*

Understanding the Format: Each category of design capability (Design as Aesthetics, Design as Usability, Design as Experience, Design as Operations, Design as Strategy, and Design as a Force for Good) includes five statements, such as *"Design adapts seamlessly to different devices and screen sizes."* These statements describe specific competencies or practices within that category.

Confidence Rating: For each category, you will respond to the five statements. Rate your confidence level in delivering on each statement using the following scale:

Rating Scale:

1 = Not Confident

2 = Slightly Confident

3 = Moderately Confident

4 = Very Confident

5 = Extremely Confident

Steps to Complete the Assessment
Carefully review each of the five statements in each category. For each statement, assign a score between 1 and 5 based on your confidence in your ability to deliver on that statement.
Calculate the Average for the Category:
Within each category, average the scores you assigned to each of the five questions.

What Do the Scores Mean?

Between 1 and 2 points (average score per category):
This score indicates low confidence in the organization's ability to deliver in this area. Significant improvement is needed to build the skills, processes, and strategies necessary to perform well. The organization may have limited resources or experience in this category and should prioritize foundational development.

Between 2 and 3 points (average score per category):

A score in this range reflects moderate confidence, suggesting that the organization has begun to take steps in this category but faces challenges in consistently delivering results. There may be gaps in processes or resources, and further development is needed to strengthen the organization's ability to perform effectively.

Between 3 and 4 points (average score per category):

At this level, the organization shows reasonable confidence in its ability to deliver in this category. Progress has been made, and there are established practices, though there may still be areas requiring fine tuning to achieve higher performance and alignment with business goals.

Between 4 and 5 points (average score per category):

This score suggests high confidence in delivering within this area. The organization has developed robust processes and systems that support effective execution. At this level, the focus might shift to exploring innovative ways to push boundaries further.

But scores alone can be abstract; to lend credibility to these ratings, there's a column for citing specific examples of practice. This serves a dual purpose:

- Validation: It's easy to agree with a statement in principle, but such agreement should be anchored in tangible experiences. For instance, while a company might assert they prioritize user experience, if they can't cite examples of feedback mechanisms they've instituted or how they've iterated based on user feedback, it brings into question the depth of their commitment to user experience.

- Richer Insights: Providing examples allows for a more nuanced understanding of the ratings. It can help in distinguishing between organizations at the initial stages of a level vs. those that have deeply ingrained a particular design practice.

This dual-pronged approach—ratings complemented by real-world examples—ensures a rigorous and insightful assessment process.

Map Your Results: Once you have calculated the average scores for each of the six categories, plot these scores onto a radar chart (Figure 1-4). Each axis of the diagram represents a category, and the plot will visually illustrate your organization's strengths and areas for improvement across the design capabilities.

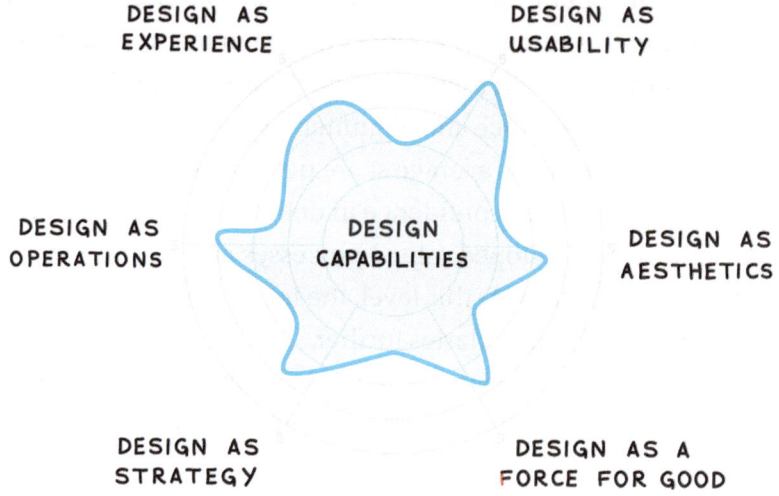

Figure 1-4. *Visualization of mapping your design capability onto a radar chart*

Understanding confidence levels can inform strategic decisions about where to invest in design resources or training, ensuring efforts are directed toward the most impactful areas.

The scoring ranges for the design capabilities assessment help us to understand the depth and breadth of an organization's design capabilities. Companies are encouraged to develop a broad range of skills and knowledge—these can range from foundational aesthetics to societal and environmental impact.

Rather than progressing through maturity levels, organizations can develop and prioritize design categories based on their strategic needs. Different organizations have different needs, and not every company needs to excel in all six categories to succeed. For example, an ecommerce company like Amazon is highly focused on usability and operational efficiency. Their design strategy prioritizes convenience, accessibility, and operational excellence (think AWS, same-day delivery), whereas a consumer electronics company like Apple might put a higher emphasis on design aesthetics and design strategy.

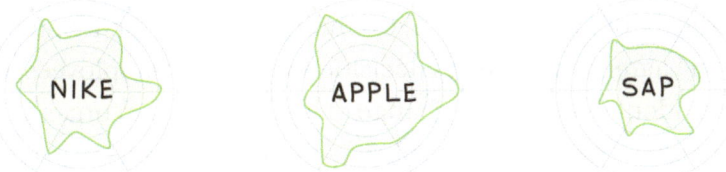

Figure 1-5. *How the capability score might vary across companies*

A company doesn't need to aim for 5's in every category. Where might 3's be acceptable? A sports apparel company like Nike might prioritize design as aesthetics and design as strategy. On the other hand, SaaS companies like SAP could be comfortable with 3s in categories like aesthetics or force for good (Figure 1-5). For SaaS companies, operational efficiency and usability are critical, but aesthetics may not play as large a role, and their "Force for Good" initiatives might not be a key part of their identity or value proposition to clients.

A tailored approach ensures that organizations focus on enhancing the capabilities that matter most to their success. Unlike design maturity models which often suggest a standardized progression, an effective design capability assessment should acknowledge that different companies have unique priorities and values. Design capabilities should align with what is right for their specific context.

Figure 1-6. *Evaluating design capabilities against competitors or industry leaders*

Recognizing the team's unique strengths and weaknesses can help them navigate change. Leadership changes within organizations like Elon Musk's takeover of Twitter (now X) exemplify the need for adaptability. Whether one agrees with Musk's decision to fire 7,500 employees at Twitter or not, it's undeniable that any change of leadership in an organization can be disruptive.[5] Such changes often bring about rapid shifts in priorities and strategies. Teams with more well-rounded capabilities are typically more resilient in the face of these changes. A solid understanding of how their capabilities stack up allows them to respond more effectively to change.

Success of Measures

 Martin Slaughter is a cofounder of a specialist management consultancy and over 45 years of experience in Operations Research—a complex branch of applied mathematics— quantifying problems and using continuing assessment to track and guide change. He has worked with corporations, charities, and governments worldwide.

(*continued*)

---

[5] Siddiqui, Faiz, "Musk's Twitter Investors Have Lost Billions in Value," The Washington Post, 1 Sept. 2024, www.washingtonpost.com/ technology/2024/09/01/musk-twitter-investors-underwater/.

Success of Measures

The maxim shared by all good carpenters—"measure twice, cut once"—is readily extendable to cover anything we do in life. It underlines the importance of carefully considering your design and marking it up before you brandish your saw. In other words, make sure you know what you need to do before you do it.

Change programs are rarely as simple as carpentry. They involve many tools and internal (and often external) factors can change the design as you try to implement it. However, measuring helps to clarify what needs to be done, what progress is being made, and where corrective action is required. To improve on our maxim, we might say "measure, saw, repeat."

Any program needs to start with an initial assessment. If you don't know where you are, then how can you plan to get to where you want to be? This measurement needs to be in terms of what success looks like, not just what you do/know now. Indeed, the process of deciding what to measure to know objectively how you are doing is a powerful exercise.

At this stage, there is a temptation to press ahead, assuming that if you follow the plan, you are guaranteed success. Experience, however, shows it is common to complete the initial plan without achieving the desired benefits—and quite often missing some tricks in the process.

It is better to design your assessment criteria so that they have readily measurable metrics and to monitor these as you deliver the program. This provides reassurance that the expected benefits are being achieved and allows divergence from expected progress to be spotted, understood, and corrected.

(continued)

Success of Measures

A salient example involves the roll-out of technology in a government organization in the UK. The delivery schedule was running on time, and so, from a purely numerical standpoint, the program was succeeding. However, our metrics showed that the expected benefits (in terms of rebalancing use of work time) were not being achieved. The metrics allowed us to identify that this was because the equipment wasn't being used as intended. This was attributable to incorrect usage by supervisory staff, influencing their teams to follow suit. Armed with this information, the program team could tackle the cultural issue and the measurements showed a rapid rise in the realization of the intended benefits.

The moral of the story is, the right measures of success lead to the success of your measures!

—Martin Slaughter

Elevating Design Ops Through Strategic Linkages

The integration of design into an organization's strategic framework is crucial for steering clear of the "one-hit wonder" phenomenon, where a specific design initiative appears to succeed solely because Venus happened to be in retrograde. In the past, design operations functioned independently, directed at maximizing workflow efficiency on a by-project basis. While this bottom-up approach was effective in terms of operational efficacy and efficiency, it ensured there was no executive visibility into the design's contributions.

This golden thread of visibility requires going beyond isolated design metrics and instead utilizing tools capable of mapping initiatives to wider enterprise goals. For maximum impact, design operations should be elevated from merely operational to strategic and deeply embedded into the organization's culture. Achieving this involves creating a link between design operations and overarching business strategies, aided by tools such as those found in this book.

24

Strategic Challenges in Design Operations:

- Linking Operations with Strategy: The primary challenge is to transform design operations from being perceived solely as providing an operational function to also contributing strategy. How can our design efforts be aligned with and actively support overarching business objectives?

- Balancing Process and Creativity: While design operations focus mainly on streamlining processes, it's essential to ensure these processes foster rather than stifle creativity. The strategic question here is how to create systems that support operational efficiency without sacrificing creative innovation.

- User-Centricity vs. Business Objectives: Often centered on user experience, design efforts need to be better aligned with business goals. It's about finding the strategic intersection where user-centric design drives business value.

- Scalability within Strategic Frameworks: As an organization evolves, so too should its design operations, not just in scale but in strategic scope. The challenge is to adapt our methods and processes to fit an ever-evolving strategic environment.

- Measuring Strategic Impact: Beyond operational metrics, defining and measuring the strategic impact of design operations is vital. This involves identifying metrics that reflect its operational efficacy and efficiency along with its contribution to business outcomes.

- Cultural Integration: Embedding Design Operations into the organizational culture to align with and support the company's mission and strategic goals is crucial. This integration fosters a design-centric mindset across the organization, enhancing team collaboration, encouraging innovation, and leading to more effective service delivery to customers.

Bridging Design and Strategy with a Unified Framework

In many modern organizations, especially those without a traditional design focus, there's often a lack of appropriate tools, processes, and frameworks that can align design initiatives to an organization's broader goals or their market performance. This can lead to a significant misalignment, where the output of design teams might not align with what the organization requires to thrive in the market.

While existing design frameworks, such as Pirate Metrics—Acquisition, Activation, Retention, Referral, Revenue (AARRR)—and HEART—Happiness, Engagement, Adoption, Retention, Task success—offer insights into user behavior metrics and user experiences, respectively, they often overlook broader strategic challenges an organization faces. On the other end of the spectrum, established business strategy frameworks like Porter's Five Forces or the Balanced Scorecard offer strategic analysis but lack a focus on the specific role and impact of design.

This is where the TRACES framework contributes to the growing body of work in strategic design.

Here's what each area entails:

Technical Debt: This refers to short-term compromises that, although they may work now, create long-term technical problems. In other words, opting for a quick, less robust solution today can lead to large-scale breakdowns tomorrow. And if this debt is not "repaid" with maintenance or course correction, it can accumulate "interest," often making it progressively harder to implement changes.

Regulatory Changes: This involves staying aware of the ongoing legal and regulatory environment that might affect your design or product. Changes in regulations, such as privacy laws, environmental standards, or industry-specific rules, can significantly impact how a company operates and what adjustments need to be made to stay compliant.

Audience Shift: This is the recognition that customer preferences, demographics, and behaviors change over time. Businesses need to track their target audience as they evolve and adjust their strategies accordingly to maintain relevance and appeal.

Competition: This area highlights the need to monitor and respond to changes in the competitive landscape. New companies arise, companies merge, and shifts in market capitalization can affect a business's positioning. Understanding how competitors are innovating and evolving is crucial to maintaining or growing market share.

Economic Trends: Economic conditions like inflation, interest rates, or broader economic cycles influence consumer behavior and business operations. Being prepared for economic changes helps companies adapt and stay resilient during downturns or capitalize during periods of growth.

Substitute Technologies: This refers to innovations or alternative technologies that can disrupt an industry or make your product outdated or even obsolete. Keeping an eye on emerging technologies ensures you stay competitive by either adopting new solutions or pivoting your business model to avoid being displaced by more advanced alternatives.

TRACES: Elevating Design Ops to Strategic Relevance

TRACES represents an evolutionary step from Design Operations to Design Strategy, shifting the focus from solely operational efficiency to a broader, strategic context. Rather than replacing Design Operations, TRACES complements and enhances it by offering a framework that enriches the strategic aspects of design decision-making. It provides a broader perspective, enabling design leaders to align their operational choices with larger business goals and market dynamics. This complementary nature of TRACES stems from its ability to integrate key external factors into the operational framework of design.

Understanding the TRACES-Informed Strategy

The TRACES-Informed Strategy (Table 1-1) is a versatile framework that goes beyond traditional management approaches by integrating multiple dimensions of decision-making by addressing tactical and strategic challenges of design. This framework helps companies align short-term goals with future vision, ensuring a culture of innovation that is resilient to market fluctuations and economic uncertainty. Leaders can use this framework to make progress in solving granular, day-to-day challenges and demonstrating quick wins while maintaining a clear focus on the big wins necessary to achieving the company's long-term, strategic goals.

Table 1-1. *TRACES-Informed Strategy*

Type	Strategic management and composite measurement framework
Scope	Cross-functional—encompassing technical, legal, market, economic, and innovation considerations.
Application	Primarily applicable to Design Strategy but also relevant to product management, marketing, innovation, and strategic planning.
Level	Integrates tactical and strategic thinking, addressing immediate concerns and long-term planning.

Leveraging TRACES for Strategic Alignment

The evolution of design in the corporate world has traditionally centered on operational excellence—mastering tasks, delving into user personas, and crafting intricate design elements. This focus formed the foundation of captivating user interfaces and experiences. But as design has matured, it's clear that just having operational expertise isn't enough for today's business challenges.

In most organizations, design starts small, maybe with one designer or a small team, and over time, expands. This grassroots growth in design, while nurturing innovation and adaptability, often presents challenges in shifting toward a more strategic focus.

This is where the TRACES framework is invaluable. TRACES empowers design leaders to speak in a strategic language within their organizations, aligning the design function with broader business strategies. It ensures that design practice not only drives decision-making but is also embedded as a key driver in achieving the organization's overarching goals.

- Strategic Focus: TRACES empowers design teams to anticipate and respond to evolving challenges and opportunities, fostering a forward-thinking strategy in design.

- Alignment with Business Goals: By factoring in elements like competition, economic trends, and regulatory shifts, TRACES guides design efforts to align closely with the broader business objectives of the organization.

- User-Centric Approach: TRACES incorporates audience shifts as a key focus area, ensuring that design strategies are firmly rooted in user needs and behaviors. This helps designers to adapt in response to how audiences interact with and perceive products and services.

- Innovation and Agility: The framework highlights substitute technologies and technical debt, encouraging ongoing innovation and adaptability, and enables organizations to stay ahead of disruption in the rapidly evolving tech landscape.

- Risk Management: By identifying potential risks stemming from regulatory compliance to competitive landscapes, TRACES supports informed and robust decision-making in design strategies.

- Synergy with Existing Methodologies: TRACES complements and enhances existing methodologies, such as Agile, Lean UX, and Design Thinking. It acts as a strategic overlay, enriching these methodologies for greater effectiveness and strategic relevance.

The TRACES framework offers a multifaceted approach for strategic decision-making in modern design operations. This approach bridges the gap between design, business strategy, technological change, and user preferences, ensuring decisions contribute effectively to the organization's goals and strategies that can adapt to continuously evolving business environments.

Key Takeaways

- The role and perception of design in organizations have evolved from an initial focus on aesthetics and functionality to a more strategic function integrated across business objectives.

- Design is transitioning away from being viewed as merely a cost center to recognition as a value creator that drives competitive differentiation, user satisfaction, and revenue growth for organizations.

- Design in organizations can be elevated by creating clear linkages between design operations and corporate strategy, ensuring alignment with business objectives.

- New business tools, frameworks, and methodologies like TRACES can help bridge the gap between design and organizational strategy by providing a strategic view encompassing technical, regulatory, market, economic, and innovation considerations.

- The TRACES framework equips design leaders with a holistic strategic perspective that aligns design efforts with business goals, user needs, innovation imperatives, and risk management.

PART I

Do Things Better

"Less, but better."

—Dieter Rams

How do we optimize our resources to create more efficient design operations? It starts with setting a clear strategic direction. First, we need to establish clarity around the organization's vision and goals. Are we aiming for growth, maintenance, or a mix of both? Once we've decided, it's important to communicate this direction across all levels of the organization. When everyone is on the same page, they can make informed decisions that support these objectives. This alignment streamlines efforts and drives continuous improvement, empowering teams to focus on work that creates value and directly contributes to the organization's strategic goals.

The TRACES Framework offers strategic insights using a thorough method to assess opportunity and risk. They can help companies justify design choices more rigorously, making it easier to demonstrate value. How do these changes impact your business now and in the future? What do they mean for your overall strategy? Organizations need to adapt quickly to stay ahead, and design operations—with their inherent flexibility and creativity—should lead this charge, acting as the tip of the spear.

The TRACES Framework brings product development, user experience, and brand identity insights into sharper focus by connecting them to strategic goals. This ensures that design operations actively support the company's overarching goals and drive the organization toward its goals. By embracing these principles, organizations become more aligned, adaptable, and innovative, enabling them to respond to change and move forward with greater confidence.

CHAPTER 2

Laying the Groundwork

Where are we going, and how will we get there? These fundamental questions shape a company's vision and define its strategy for success. For over a century, Disney—one of the most enduring and impactful companies—has provided quality entertainment for families. It wasn't by accident. Walt Disney had a clear vision from the beginning. He knew to achieve his goal he had to build an animation studio, create theme parks, and hire top talent to produce quality entertainment. Walt Disney strictly enforced his vision and ensured that everybody at the company knew their role. This vision was so strong it has far outlived Walt Disney and remains a part of the company's DNA. The Disney company protects their IP like a dog protects his bone, and their strict rules on safety in their theme parks are legendary.

Not every leader has a vision as far-reaching as Walt Disney's, but they still need to know where they are going and how they plan to get there. A lack of conviction around this question can result in misaligned teams and departments who pull in opposite directions or jockey for power where boundaries are ill-defined. These conflicting priorities lead to inefficiencies and wasted resources that will ultimately impact the bottom line. Design teams might be pressured to pursue projects that seem exciting or valuable in isolation but don't support the bigger picture of the company's overall strategy. Therefore, before we can align design with business objectives, we must first determine our overall direction and approach.

© Garkay Wong 2025
G. Wong, *The Art of Design Strategy*, Design Thinking,
https://doi.org/10.1007/979-8-8688-0552-3_2

In this chapter, you will learn

- The challenges and risks associated with misalignment

- How to define your Strategic posture (Maintenance vs. Growth)

- How to use the Strategy Alignment Canvas to link design projects to business goals

Building a Strong Foundation for Alignment

Choosing a path forward is only the beginning. Once a strategic direction is set, this brings us to our next question: *Are the stakeholders in the organization aligned with this direction?* For real change to happen, your people must be on board. This is where the tone from senior leaders plays a defining role. To steer corporate growth and innovation through uncertainty, it's not enough to say, "This is the direction." Employees need to feel that the strategy is backed by genuine commitment, and leaders need to nurture a culture that encourages change. When all levels of the organization are aligned with strategic goals, teams can move together with purpose, allowing everyone to contribute meaningfully to those objectives.

In principle, it's a no-brainer that design initiatives should visibly link to the company's strategy. However, design initiatives and business goals can often be in conflict, as illustrated in Figure 2-1. In practice, this alignment can be one of the hardest things to achieve. With too many constraints, innovation is killed before it gets traction. Too few constraints and we may get radical ideas that seem exciting and different but are neither practical nor feasible to implement. Good design delivers both. It balances creative approaches to problem-solving with achievable solutions by making the best use of the resources available.

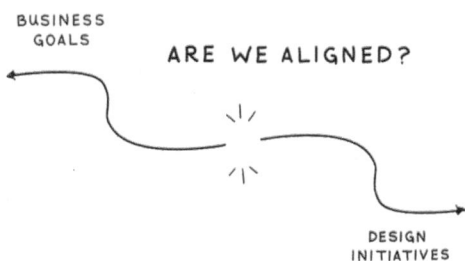

Figure 2-1. *Are we aligned?*

One example of how this conflict can play out between business goals and design initiatives is the case of Apple's Project Titan. In 2014, Apple was a household name synonymous with innovation. They were known for creating groundbreaking products like the iPod, iPhone, iPad, and MacBook. Following this string of successes and Steve Jobs' passing, Apple decided it was time to disrupt yet another industry. This time around, it would take on the automotive industry with the goal of revolutionizing the way people drive. Thus, Project Titan was born.

However, as with any transformative project, the journey was far from smooth. Internal disputes developed immediately, centering on the project's direction. *Should Apple develop a fully autonomous vehicle, capable of navigating the roads without any human intervention? Or should the company take a more measured approach, creating a semi-autonomous car that combines advanced technology with traditional driving controls?* Steve Zadesky, the Apple executive initially in charge of Project Titan, wanted to pursue the semi-autonomous option. However, industrial design team members, including Jony Ive, Apple's chief designer, believed a fully driverless car would allow the company to upend the automobile experience.[1]

---

[1] Potuck, Michael, "Report: Apple's Car Project 'Titan' went from reinventing the (spherical) wheel to just a PAIL/carOS," 9to5Mac, August 22, 2017, https://9to5mac.com/2017/08/22/project-titan-what-happened/.

As years passed, Project Titan saw numerous changes in leadership and strategic direction, leading to instability and uncertainty within the project. All the way up until its cancellation in early 2024, Project Titan was mired in what is known in the software industry as "development hell," a term used to describe a project that faces ongoing delays and "seems to be stuck in development forever."[2] Project Titan was scaled back and reprioritized so often that you'd be forgiven for thinking that maybe it should've been named Project Sisyphus.

The project never managed to overcome continual delays, leadership changes, and staffing turbulence—resulting in multiple rounds of layoffs and rehiring to accommodate a constantly shifting vision. This demonstrates how misalignment between vision, leadership, and execution can derail major design initiatives, as shown in Figure 2-2. When major design initiatives fail to align around broader corporate priorities, it can lead to extended timelines, bloated budgets, and employee attrition.

THE PRICE OF MISALIGNMENT

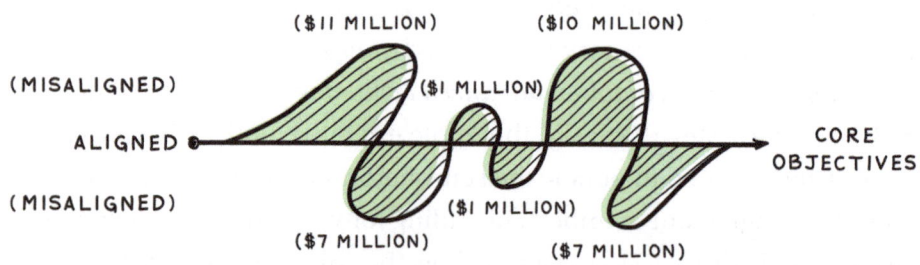

Figure 2-2. *The price of misalignment*

[2] Leblanc, Wesley, "Video Games Stuck in Development Hell Part 1," Game Informer, 1 Nov. 2021, https://web.archive.org/web/20211106053408/ https://www.gameinformer.com/2021/11/01/video-games-stuck-in-development-hell-part-1.

In hindsight, Project Titan likely suffered from disagreement between how much change Apple was prepared to support and how much change the project's lofty goals required. Perhaps the project strayed too far from Apple's mission "to bring the best user experience to customers through innovative hardware, software, and services."[3] The overly ambitious nature of the project clashed with the company's readiness to fully embrace the necessary changes, and the more the project diverged over time, the greater the disconnect became, resulting in design efforts that fell entirely out of step with the company's overall strategy.

So, how do you ensure that this doesn't happen at your organization? Well, since we know that reaping the benefits of design initiatives can take time, embedding continuous sense checks to ensure that design initiatives haven't strayed too far from the big picture is crucial to realizing those benefits.

The TRACES Growth Matrix

The TRACES Growth Matrix helps you understand the overall landscape of your design initiatives in relation to business objectives and provides decision support. How much are you willing to push beyond your current capabilities to achieve the desired benefits? What is the degree of change required? Should the change be incremental or radically transformative? While everyone might agree that some level of change is necessary, the real debate is about an organization's appetite for change—how much and how rapidly it should occur—rather than whether it should happen at all.

The appetite for change impacts how we navigate this alignment. Bringing design initiatives into alignment with broader organizational strategy is no easy feat. Misalignment can arise when there is disagreement about a chosen direction or the level of change required to achieve the

---

[3] Pereira, Daniel, "Apple Mission and Vision Statement," Business Model Analyst, August 27, 2024, https://businessmodelanalyst.com/apple-mission-and-vision-statement/.

desired outcome. The TRACES Growth Matrix—as shown in Figure 2-3—is a tool for facilitating productive discussions around the portfolio of design initiatives and ensuring those initiatives stay true to the organization's strategic direction.

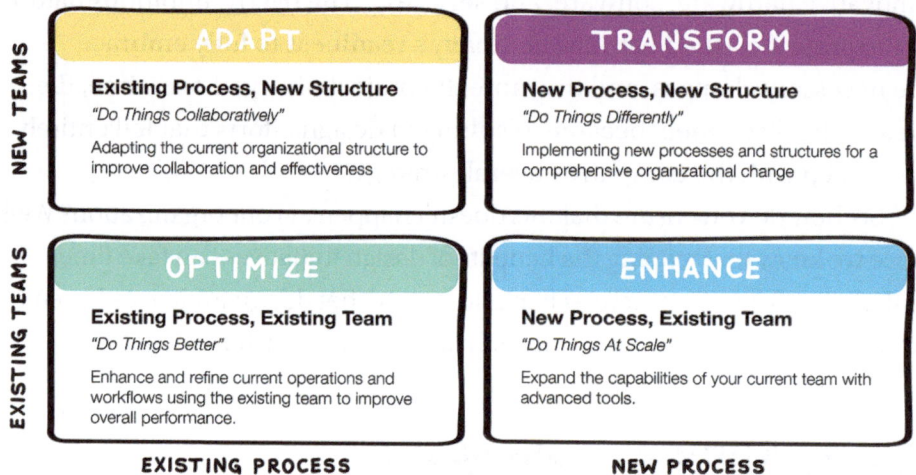

Figure 2-3. *TRACES Growth Matrix*

Delivering on initiatives without a clearly defined strategy in place puts design leaders at risk of producing wrong outcomes. The TRACES Growth Matrix's four quadrants—Optimize, Enhance, Adapt, and Transform—address different aspects of a company's growth strategy to ensure that projects are executed under a cohesive plan. Leadership can ensure that their efforts are driving the company in the intended direction. Whether by optimizing existing resources, enhancing technical capabilities with new tools, adapting new team structures, or undergoing a transformation that involves new business models, each quadrant offers a targeted perspective on key areas of improvement. For instance, asset-intensive companies like airlines often benefit from concentrating their efforts in the Optimize quadrant to maximize the value derived from each of their assets. This is because their core assets are extremely costly to replace and reconfigure, which makes frequent transformation unlikely. In contrast, a software company may adopt a more transformative approach to stay competitive. Ultimately, a successful design approach requires that the chosen strategy is aligned to the appropriate degree of change for the organization.

Design initiatives can be mapped to one of four quadrants using common terms like Optimize, Enhance, Adapt, and Transform (Table 2-1). Each quadrant broadly reflects the direction and degree of change required. The tool can be used to assess a portfolio of design initiatives and foster meaningful dialogue around the alignment of plans and strategies.

Table 2-1. *Overview of the four strategic approaches of the TRACES Growth Matrix*

Strategy	Description
Optimize (Existing Process, Existing Teams)	*"Do Things Better"* Improve operations with the current team and processes for efficiency
Enhance (New Process, Existing Teams)	*"Do Things at Scale"* Enhance team capabilities with advanced tools
Adapt (Existing Process, New Structure)	*"Do Things Collaboratively"* Modify structure for better collaboration with existing processes
Transform (New Process, Existing Structure)	*"Do Things Differently"* Overhaul processes and structures for major change

Alignment on a Strategic Posture: Maintenance vs. Growth

For most companies under normal circumstances, the maintenance posture is the safest choice. Optimizing existing teams and processes is a low-cost way of making improvements while reducing risks (no need to invest much additional capital or resources). On the other hand, the three growth-oriented pathways—investing in new technologies, teams, or business models—require greater spending and carry more risk but create possibilities for substantial growth and transformation. Table 2-2 summarizes these four postures.

Table 2-2. *Organizational risk levels for strategic growth*

Posture	Strategy	Risk
Maintain	**Optimize** (Existing Process, Existing Teams)	Low
Grow	**Enhance** (New Process, Existing Teams)	Moderate
Grow	**Adapt** (Existing Process, New Structure)	Moderate
Grow	**Transform** (New Process, New Structure)	High

Maintenance Posture in Design

On average, many companies tend to operate in the Optimization quadrant, squeezing out additional efficiencies here and there and generally playing on the margins. If there is no strategic imperative driving the need for major change, companies may find maintaining the status quo preferable. This applies when the business environment appears stable, the company is performing well, and there's no immediate threat or opportunity requiring a shift in strategy.

While maintaining the status quo can be tempting, even in a stable market, complacency can leave a company vulnerable. Depending on the volatility of external forces, over-indexing on this approach can restrict a company's growth potential and its ability to adapt, making it more vulnerable to disruption.

Optimize (Existing Process, Existing Teams): "Do Things Better"

Cost Implications: Optimization—in the context of adopting a maintenance posture—is a cost-effective strategy for companies looking to maximize their current resources. By refining workflows and enhancing established methodologies across the organization, leaders can drive improvements without prohibitively expensive financial investment. The emphasis here is on making incremental changes that drive cost saving, potentially increasing the return on investment (ROI) with minimal additional expenditure.

The Optimize approach involves streamlining operational processes. It involves finding better ways to leverage existing resources, boost efficiency, and improve performance. Characterized by its cautious, risk-averse nature, this approach values stability and gradual improvements. While this optimization path is favored for its promise of predictable outcomes and relatively low risk, it can inadvertently hinder the organization's ability to adapt quickly in response to emerging challenges.

Growth Posture in Design

Teams embracing a growth posture must recognize the heightened stakes involved and plan for strategic adjustments. Existing capabilities may not be sufficient or there might not be enough capacity to take on a big transformation project. New competencies will need to be developed gradually, meaning sustained investments need to be made over the long term. If you're a budget holder, this is already setting off the alarm bells in your head.

Teams embracing a growth posture to align with the strategic initiative owner(s) to ensure their investments are directed toward achieving these goals. Clear objectives, careful planning, and adequate investments are necessary for a successful growth strategy. Having effective progress tracking, proper resource allocation, and risk mitigation plans in place helps prevent the strategy from falling apart. This is a lot to consider (I didn't say this would be easy), but unless most, if not all, these elements are in place, the entire growth strategy risks collapsing into chaos.

Beyond process and planning, a key risk to consider is change fatigue. Too much change in a short period can overwhelm employees. Recognizing the symptoms of change fatigue is the first step toward addressing it effectively. One of the most apparent symptoms is emotional exhaustion. Employees may feel drained and stressed, struggling to find the energy to tackle their daily tasks. This exhaustion stems from the continuous mental and emotional effort required to adjust to new ways of working, often without adequate time to recover from previous changes.

Unfortunately, there is no precise way of measuring emotional exhaustion. You just need to be on the watch for how employees respond to the stresses of change. Identifying this early allows leaders to intervene before the situation worsens. By addressing the root causes of change fatigue, organizations can maintain a healthy, productive work environment even amid necessary transitions.

As you can see, a Growth approach inherently carries higher risk. But higher risk can mean a higher reward. Pushing these boundaries can open a world of transformative opportunities. Below, we discuss the growth posture quadrants and how they provide direction for organizations in their strategic initiatives.

Enhance (New Process, Existing Team): "Do Things at Scale"

Cost Implications: While introducing new design processes or tools involves some level of investment, it doesn't require the costs associated with building new teams. Design leaders can focus on enhancing the capabilities of their existing teams, integrating innovative design methodologies, or adopting new technologies. This approach is a balanced option, offering a way to innovate within a reasonable budget, enhancing the team's capabilities without extensive restructuring costs.

Adapt (Existing Process, New Structure): "Do Things Collaboratively"

Cost Implications: This strategy involves modifying team structures or creating new collaborative units across the organization. It could include various models, such as embedded design teams, consulting or in-sourcing approaches, or decentralized outcome-oriented teams that focus on solving specific problems rather than adhering to strict reporting lines. This approach to change involves adapting team structures to specific objectives while keeping processes constant. Achieving this may require investment in training, increasing collaboration between departments, or forming external partnerships. The associated costs include both financial implications and the time required for change which can be significant but manageable with careful planning. Design leaders should consider how new team structures can lead to a more engaged workforce, foster effective teams, and enhance the prominence of the design function—all of which contribute to the overall success and resilience of the organization. This should be balanced against the need to manage the associated costs and challenges with adapting these team structures to ensure that change sticks.

Transform (New Processes, New Structure): "Do Things Differently"

Cost Implications: Transformation, the most ambitious and resource-intensive option, requires a complete overhaul of processes and team structures. Design leaders considering this route must prepare for significant investments in new technologies, training, and hiring. It's a high-risk, high-reward strategy that can propel a design department into new heights of innovation, but requires careful planning and a substantial commitment of resources to succeed.

Although pursuing any of the growth strategies is necessary for driving innovation, leaders must be aware of the risks they carry. Any change initiative can potentially impact existing corporate objectives which may lead to increased scrutiny during times of economic downturn or periods of uncertainty. It is vital for design leaders and executives to recognize and strategically manage these risks. An informed approach ensures that innovative initiatives, even if they aren't central to the business at present, are undertaken with a full understanding of their potential impact and are supported by necessary contingency planning to ensure that benefits are realized.

Companies must constantly weigh the trade-offs between innovative pursuits and maintaining operational stability and profitability. Project Titan's experience is a reminder that while pursuing innovation is essential for growth, it requires a careful, well-thought-out approach to align with the overall goals of the company.

As a design leader, recognizing when and how to advocate for strategic change is crucial. This involves identifying opportunities where innovation can significantly impact the organization's future trajectory.

Preparing for Strategic Alignment Discussions

- **Understand and Articulate Corporate Objectives:** A designer needs to deeply understand their company's strategic goals and how they translate to various business functions, and specifically how they fit into the overall plan.

- **Categorize Design Initiatives:** Organize ongoing and planned design projects into the Strategic Growth Matrix quadrants (Optimize, Enhance, Adapt, Transform). Assess each initiative's current alignment with the company's strategic goals.

  - **Optimize (Existing Process, Existing Teams):** "Do Things Better." Enhance and refine operations and workflows using the existing team for incremental improvements and efficiency gains. For example, a design change that reduces the complexity of service requests can lead to a decrease in call center volume and free up customer support resources to focus on more complex issues and strategic customer engagement.

  - **Enhance (New Process, Existing Team):** "Do Things at Scale." Expand the capabilities of the current team by investing in new tools and processes. For example, implementing a new collaborative communication tool for teams.

  - **Adapt (Existing Process, New Structure):** "Do Things Collaboratively." Adapt the organizational structure to improve collaboration and effectiveness. One way to foster better collaboration could involve reorganizing teams into cross-functional squads combining subject matter experts, designers, developers, and product managers working together on specific features.

  - **Transform (New Processes, New Structure):** "Do Things Differently." Implement new processes and structures for comprehensive organizational change. For example, a brick-and-mortar store changing its business model to be ecommerce based.

- **Prepare to Communicate Strategic Alignment**

  - **Aligned Initiatives:** Be ready to show how design projects align with and support immediate strategic goals.

  - **Misaligned Initiatives:** For misaligned projects, explain to stakeholders why they should be dropped.

Practical Application: The Strategy Alignment Canvas

The Strategy Alignment Canvas aligns design initiatives with the overarching goals of a business. Its purpose is to ensure that design efforts directly contribute to strategic objectives. This canvas acts as a guide for teams to visualize and assess how their design projects support broader business goals.

Key Benefits of the Canvas:

- **Alignment of Design Initiatives with Business Goals:**

  The canvas serves as a tool to align design projects with the overarching goals of the business. This ensures that design efforts directly contribute to the strategic objectives.

- **Visual Mapping:**

  The canvas allows design and business leaders to visually map out the current position of their initiatives in relation to the company's broader strategy. This visual representation aids in understanding and communicating the expected business benefits of design projects.

- **Assessment of Design Relevance:**

  The canvas provides a framework to assess the relevance of design initiatives with business goals. This helps to determine whether the design projects are optimally contributing to the strategic approach.

- **Strategic Approaches:**

  Design projects and company objectives are mapped onto four strategic approaches: Optimize, Enhance, Adapt, and Transform. This categorization helps in understanding how design initiatives fit into the larger strategic plan and in identifying areas for improvement or change.

Strategy Alignment Canvas

In boardrooms across the world, senior leaders and key stakeholders hold critical meetings to decide the future of their companies. These meetings, often held once a quarter, are highly consequential. They can amplify successes or failures; good performance can gain additional buy-in from the board and clear blockers, while poor results can result in the withdrawal of support and possible job loss for an unlucky executive. One way to ensure the company is going in the right direction is with the Strategy Alignment Canvas.

The Strategy Alignment Canvas (Figure 2-4) is a tool to align design initiatives with business goals. It situates design projects and company objectives within four strategic approaches and allows design and business leaders to visually map out where their initiatives stand in relation to the company's broader strategy and to assess whether they are relevant.

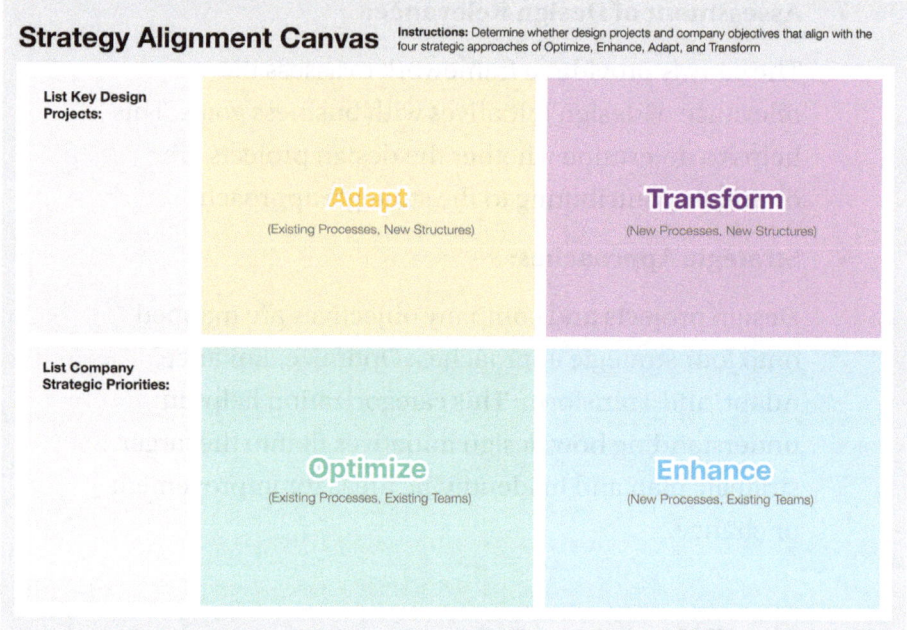

Figure 2-4. *Strategy Alignment Canvas*

Components of the Strategy Alignment Canvas

Here are the components of the Strategy Alignment Canvas:

- **List Company Strategic Priorities:** Here, we engage senior leaders and other key stakeholders to collectively define the key strategic priorities of the company.

- **List Key Design Projects:** This section is for identifying and listing main design initiatives or projects currently underway or planned.

- **Four Strategic Quadrants:**

  - *Optimize:* Projects in this quadrant focus on enhancing and refining existing processes and workflows using current teams. They aim for incremental improvements and efficiency gains.

  - *Enhance:* This quadrant involves expanding the capabilities of the current team to adapt to new processes, thereby doing existing things in new ways.

  - *Adapt:* Involves adapting the organizational structure to improve collaboration and effectiveness while maintaining existing processes.

  - *Transform:* Represents comprehensive organizational change, implementing new processes and structures for major pivots.

Alignment: The Design Strategist's North Star

Neil Williams is a seasoned design strategist, service designer and human centered design (HCD) practitioner with over 20 years of experience leading multidisciplinary teams in Asia. Specializing in digital, spatial, and narrative design, he has driven significant business transformation across diverse sectors. Neil has enhanced customer experiences for major corporations and cultural institutions and regularly shares his insights on design and innovation through workshops, articles, and speaking engagements.

(continued)

Alignment: The Design Strategist's North Star

In my three decades of experience across various industries, I've come to recognize that alignment is the cornerstone of successful design strategy. This is particularly true when working in or with large multinational corporations, where misalignment is often the norm rather than the exception, especially in complex projects with significant potential impact.

Organizations are dynamic entities, and misalignment can occur at any stage due to various factors: change of leadership, shifting priorities, budget constraints, or simply the natural tension between global strategies and local needs. As a design strategist, I've found myself navigating these choppy waters time and again.

A few years ago, I found myself in the middle of a classic global–local tussle. I was working in a regional role for a major financial institution, tasked with supporting a new customer service platform. The regional headquarters had a clear vision of a streamlined, uniform system with economies of scale. However, the local entity we were working with pushed back, arguing that their unique market conditions required more flexibility.

This is where the design strategist's toolkit becomes invaluable. Our role extends beyond mere project execution; we become arbiters and facilitators of alignment, bridging local and global perspectives while zooming in and out from the macro level of vision strategy to the micro-level of nuance and application.

Here's How We Approached the Challenge

1. Stakeholder engagement: We spent time with key stakeholders from all sides to understand their perspectives, needs, and fears.

2. Visualization: We turned data, processes, and different perspectives into visual maps. This visual representation helped the regional headquarters and local offices see the bigger picture and understand each other's viewpoints.

(continued)

Alignment: The Design Strategist's North Star

3. Facilitation: We organized a series of workshops, bringing together representatives from regional and local offices. Using design thinking methodologies, we facilitated discussions that went beyond surface-level disagreements to uncover underlying needs, concerns, and opportunities.

4. Co-creation: Instead of presenting a top-down solution, we engaged stakeholders at all levels in co-creation sessions. This led to more innovative solutions and fostered a sense of ownership among all parties.

5. Continuous Engagement: We established regular check-ins and feedback loops, ensuring all voices were heard. This ongoing dialogue helped us catch and address misalignments early before they could derail the project.

The role of a strategic design leader is to build and maintain trust and alignment vertically and horizontally and to sustain the momentum needed to deliver positive impact. By leveraging our full toolkit—from visualization and facilitation skills to empathy and systems thinking—we can help organizations navigate complexity, bridge diverse perspectives, and achieve meaningful alignment.

In an increasingly globalized yet localized business environment, this ability to foster alignment while respecting diversity is not just valuable—it's essential. As design strategists, we are uniquely positioned to take on this challenge, creating bridges where we find gaps.

—Neil Williams

Workshop Introduction: Aligning Design with Corporate Strategy

Understanding the Current Situation

Your first step is to gain a clear understanding of our current situation. This involves assessing how well our design initiatives align with the company's strategic direction. Are your design efforts contributing to the company's goals? Are there discrepancies that need addressing? Alignment does not always mean conformity. Sometimes, doing things different from competitors can be a conscious choice to drive innovation and growth.

The Role of the Canvas

The canvas will guide us in evaluating whether our design initiatives are well aligned with the company's strategy. We will explore different aspects of our strategy: optimization, enhancement, adaptation, and transformation, and where our design efforts fit within these categories.

Workshop Objectives

- Evaluate Current Alignment: Assess how current design initiatives align with the company's strategic goals.

- Understand Strategic Choices: Determine the relevance and impact of current initiatives.

- Develop Actionable Strategies: Formulate concrete steps to align or realign design initiatives with the broader corporate strategy.

Participant Selection

The ideal number of participants for this workshop is between 10 to 15, which allows for a diverse range of perspectives while maintaining an environment conducive to productive discussions. For a workshop focusing on aligning the design function with the overall corporate strategy, Table 2-3 lists key participants who should be involved:

Table 2-3. *Design function workshop key players*

Department	Roles
Senior Management	Chief Operating Officer (COO)
Governance/Compliance	Chief Compliance Officer (Governance/Compliance)
Finance and Risk	CFO (Finance and Risk)
Legal	General Counsel (Legal)
Human Resources	Chief Human Resources Officer (HR)
IT	CTO (IT)
Design	Chief Design Officer (CDO)
	Senior Design Leader
Marketing	Chief Marketing Officer (Marketing)
Others (Optional)	Chief Customer Officer
	Supply Chain Management Representative (if relevant)
	Research and Development (R&D) Leader
	Product Development Manager
	Customer Relations Manager
	Operations Manager

In an ideal scenario, inviting senior leaders to participate in the alignment discussion fosters their buy-in and increases their speed of decision-making and action. In practice, however, it may not always be feasible to have senior managers present. Having them delegate representatives from the level below can still go a long way in aligning around decisions. To the extent possible, ensure that nominated representatives are knowledgeable in the topic and are expected by their superiors to make a meaningful contribution.

Preparing for the Workshop

- Materials Preparation: Prepare the alignment canvas with the TRACES Growth Matrix printed in A1 size.

- Logistics Setup: Arrange a comfortable meeting space, necessary technology, and materials. Scheduling this as a morning session is preferable to ensure the focus and attention needed for a strategic deep-thinking workshop.

- Create an agenda (Table 2-4).

Table 2-4. *Workshop agenda*

	Rundown		Time
09:30–09:45	Introduction	Overview of workshop goals and context setting	15 mins
09:45–9:50	Canvas Tool Briefing	Explain the use of the alignment canvas	5 mins
09:50–10:50	Group Mapping Activity	Group maps corporate strategy, followed by design initiatives onto the canvas.	30 mins + 30 mins
10:50–11:20	Group Presentation	Facilitate group discussion on whether the initiative(s) are desirable or beneficial.	30 mins
11:20–11:45	Strategic Alignment Review	As a group, review design initiatives and alignment with our strategic objectives to develop a prioritized list.	25 mins
11:45–12:00	Conclusion and Next Steps	Summarize insights and outline follow-up actions.	15 mins

After the Workshop

- Follow-Up: Send a follow-up email to all participants, with key insights and a summary of next steps. This helps participants feel they are part of an ongoing process rather than a "flash-in-the-pan" activity.

- Alignment Review Schedule: Establish a quarterly cadence for alignment review to track the alignment between design initiatives and business goals. Be open to adjusting the frequency based on feedback and evolving needs.

After reviewing alignment using the Strategy Alignment Canvas, the next step is to determine how and where to adjust your strategies. This is where TRACES offers valuable insights into external and internal factors that drive strategic shifts in design.

Key Takeaways

- The TRACES Growth Matrix facilitates high-level discussions on design initiative alignment, using terms like Optimize, Enhance, Adapt, and Transform to gauge if design priorities are in sync with overall business strategy.

- Companies can choose between a maintenance posture focused on cost-effective optimization of existing processes or a growth stance involving higher-risk/higher-reward innovation initiatives.

- The Strategy Alignment Canvas allows design and business leaders to visually map current design projects against strategic priorities across Optimize, Enhance, Adapt, and Transform quadrants to quickly assess and improve alignment.

CHAPTER 3

Introducing the TRACES Framework

Now that you have a clear idea of your company's direction and how you plan to get there—whether that's sticking with business as usual or following a path of growth—it's important to consider the risks that might disrupt or challenge your plan. TRACES helps you identify the risks and develop strategies to mitigate them. As you go through the process, you might find new opportunities to adjust your growth plans to ensure your approach stays aligned with your organization's shared objectives.

In this chapter, you will learn

- How to systematically identify potential threats with TRACES

- How to adapt design strategies in response to shifts in external factors

Developing a Resilient Strategy

Sonos became tremendously successful in making audio products for retail consumers. One of their major differentiators was their mobile app, which provided a seamless and intuitive user experience, allowing users

© Garkay Wong 2025
G. Wong, *The Art of Design Strategy*, Design Thinking,
https://doi.org/10.1007/979-8-8688-0552-3_3

to control audio devices across different rooms. However, a short-sighted (or perhaps poorly planned) redesign of their mobile app in 2024 led to massive backlash across its user base.

There are multiple reasons why the redesign was so poorly received, but a common thread has been a lack of user-centricity in design decisions. Yes, Sonos gathered user feedback, but this is just one of the many vectors required to gain a holistic understanding of the user context. It's not hard to imagine any number of behavioral studies, surveys, and workshops that would have led to a better-informed business decision. However expensive these studies would have been, the cost would pale in comparison to the losses incurred from this misstep. The redesign of the app was missing features, such as sleep timers and alarms, and it was very disruptive to users who had come to rely on these features in their day-to-day lives. Worse, the app became less accessible for visually impaired users with accessibility functions being reduced or completely non-functional.

To top things off with a sour cherry, after the backlash, Sonos publicly floated the idea of reintroducing the old version of its app, but had to walk this back after it was ultimately deemed infeasible due to a cross-fade of engineering resources from the old app to the new one. This is all to say that a resilient strategy—one that properly incorporates design considerations at a strategic level—could have prevented or at least mitigated the worst impacts of this decision to move to a poorly tested design.

In uncertain situations that require a resilient strategy to successfully navigate, the TRACES framework can be a very useful tool. TRACES—Technical debt, Regulatory changes, Audience shift, Competition, Economic trends, and Substitute technologies (Figure 3-1)—offers a comprehensive view of the external factors that can significantly impact your strategic direction.

TECHNICAL DEBT	REGULATORY CHANGES	AUDIENCE SHIFT	COMPETITION	ECONOMIC TRENDS	SUBSTITUTE TECHNOLOGIES
Costs from shortcuts or outdated technology	Legal requirements affecting design and scope	Evolving user needs, behaviors and preferences over time	Impact of rival companies on design strategy	Broader financial decisions influencing design choices	Emerging tech that could replace the current design

Figure 3-1. *The TRACES framework*

Integrating insights from TRACES into strategic planning allows you to anticipate and prepare for potential internal and external changes. It can help you determine whether to continue investing in optimization or to start shifting resources toward enhancing, adapting, or transforming your design practices and processes. Let's say a significant regulatory change is anticipated. It may be more strategic to preemptively move toward the "adapt" or "enhance" quadrants and invest in new processes and systems that align with the anticipated changes.

💡 Rethinking Tradition: A Brief Primer on Existing Frameworks

It's not always the case that what's commonly used is necessarily the best or most helpful. Context matters. Tools such as SWOT (Strengths, Weaknesses, Opportunities, Threats) and PEST (Political, Economic, Social, Technological) have been utilized for years to help with analysis and decision-making. They help companies assess different factors to see how they might impact the company's overall strategy.

But in today's complex world, frameworks like SWOT and PEST don't always address the most relevant threats. Indeed, trying to use old frameworks to handle modern threats would be like using an old map to navigate a modern city. While they can help to simplify our understanding of threats, they might not fit the current context. After all, these tools were created in the 1960s with stable environments in mind and may not fully address the dynamic and digital risks faced by today's businesses.

Thus, the frameworks we use must be adapted to fit the times we live in. During the 1990s, as the world became more globalized, PEST was updated to PESTLE to factor in legal and environmental aspects. Since then, information has expanded exponentially, necessitating more advanced tools to navigate markets and quickly adapt to changes in technology and consumer preferences.

TRACES presents a contemporary approach to strategic analysis by focusing on factors that organizations can actively control. Immediate threats like technical debt and audience shifts can be tackled through informed decision-making and innovation. While PESTLE factors such as political and environmental influences are important, they often lie beyond a company's influence, necessitating reactive responses rather than proactive strategies. In today's competitive environment, where customer loyalty can be easily lost by missteps, managing these factors is crucial.

TRACES emphasizes agility, enabling organizations to stay ahead by concentrating on elements they can impact rather than those they can only react to. It's not about discarding old methods but understanding that TRACES plays a role alongside traditional frameworks, complementing them with a tool tailored to current demands.

Components of the TRACES Framework

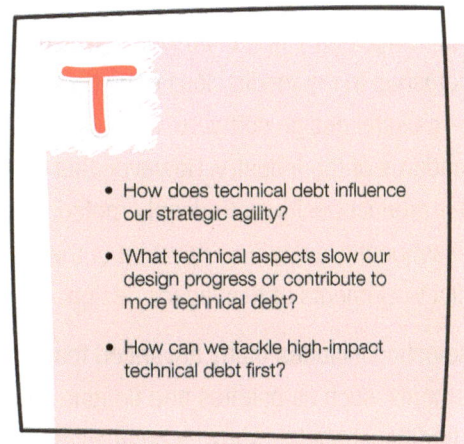

TECHNICAL
DEBT

Costs from shortcuts or
outdated technology

- How does technical debt influence our strategic agility?

- What technical aspects slow our design progress or contribute to more technical debt?

- How can we tackle high-impact technical debt first?

Technical Debt

Addressing technical debt is a cost-saving imperative. When overlooked, it accumulates, leading to higher expenses in future corrections and system overhauls. Strategically minimizing technical debt can streamline development, reduce maintenance costs, and prevent potential revenue loss from system downtimes or poor user experiences.

Questions to ask:

- How does technical debt influence our strategic agility?

- What technical aspects slow our design progress or contribute to more technical debt?

- How can we tackle high-impact technical debt first?

Technical Debt in Design and its Strategic Implications: Adobe vs. New-Age Players

As a designer, my first exposure to graphic design software was through Adobe Photoshop in my media class in high school. For decades, Adobe dominated as the go-to digital design software. Products like Photoshop and Illustrator shaped the standards of the industry. However, this extensive heritage comes with a caveat: their product designs are deeply rooted in the design paradigms of the 1990s. Consequently, every new iteration of their Creative Suite, despite improvements, still reflects elements of this legacy design.

Photoshop includes many advanced features, but it still relies on legacy design elements, such as palettes and floating windows. Tools like the "Burn" are rooted in traditional photography techniques, allowing users to darken specific areas of an image by increasing exposure.

However, there is often no clear link between these origins and the icons used today, which can confuse users. While some advanced users might prefer the classic interface, it can create a steep learning curve for newcomers who are not familiar with these photographic techniques or terminology. As a result, new users may struggle to navigate the software effectively, especially when they are accustomed to more intuitive, context-driven designs found in modern applications. Even long-time users, who've witnessed the evolution of digital interfaces now expect and demand a user experience that aligns with modern standards. Adobe's past design choices show a buildup of technical debt, where earlier decisions affect the efficiency and attractiveness of current products.

(continued)

Emergence of Figma and Canva: The Modern Vanguard

The digital design realm, however, hasn't remained static. As Adobe grapples with the burden of its history, newer entrants like Figma and Canva offer a fresh perspective. Without the constraints of legacy design and the associated technical debt, these platforms exemplify agility and modernity.

Figma's standout feature is its emphasis on real-time collaboration. Designed for the contemporary, cloud-first era, it caters to collaborative, dynamic, and immediate design. Gone are the days when designers worked in isolation, exchanging static files for feedback. With Figma, design is a living, breathing entity, allowing for instantaneous feedback and teamwork.

Canva, meanwhile, taps into a different market need: democratizing design. Recognizing that the digital age requires everyone, from entrepreneurs to educators, to occasionally don the visual designer's hat, Canva provides an intuitive platform. Its drag-and-drop interface and vast template library empower even those with no formal design training, offering a stark contrast to Adobe's technical and complex toolset.

Navigating the Landscape of Technical Debt

The paths of Adobe, Figma, and Canva reveal how technical and design debts can impact a company's strategic positioning. While legacy and history provide credibility and a solid user base, they can hinder innovation and agility. Newcomers who aren't weighed down by legacy systems can adapt quickly and disrupt the market by responding to changing user needs.

Cost of Legacy: The Silent Drift

A portion of the design community, especially those entering the field in recent years, began their journey elsewhere, not with Adobe. Every moment spent by Adobe on patching or maintaining their older system is a moment not spent on groundbreaking innovation. This creates an opportunity for new players. In this space, platforms like Figma and Canva have begun to thrive.

(continued)

Adobe is aware of the challenge, as evidenced by their attempted $20 billion acquisition of Figma (`https://www.nytimes.com/2024/02/08/technology/figma-adobe-.html`). While this acquisition was blocked by regulators, it goes to show the threat that upstarts represent to Adobe's market share. Evidently, it's a $20 billion threat (which their PR spun as an opportunity).

Adobe's journey underscores a broader industry lesson: Continuous evolution is paramount. While legacy brings with it respect and a large user base, it also carries the weight of technical debt. Recognizing, addressing, and navigating this legacy debt is necessary for organizations to maintain a strong market position.

Regulatory Changes

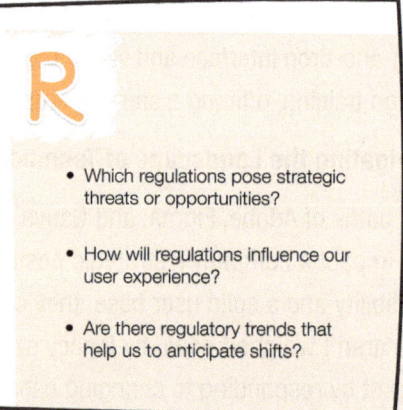

REGULATORY
CHANGES

Legal requirements
affecting design and scope

R

- Which regulations pose strategic threats or opportunities?

- How will regulations influence our user experience?

- Are there regulatory trends that help us to anticipate shifts?

Given that digital privacy and user rights are under increasing scrutiny, designers need to anticipate and accommodate regulatory shifts. For instance, Facebook has struggled under government scrutiny for how they use data. Ignoring these regulations can be a major threat, leading to significant financial penalties and damage to the company's reputation. Strategically, staying on top of these changes ensures that products stay compliant, avoiding legal issues and fines, while building trust with users.

Questions to ask:

- Which regulations pose strategic threats or opportunities?

- How will regulations influence our user experience?

- Are there regulatory trends that help us to anticipate shifts?

The GDPR Transition: Navigating Data Protection in a Digital World

Before the General Data Protection Regulation (GDPR) was introduced by the European Union (EU) in 2018, businesses had more flexibility in their approaches to gathering, managing, and utilizing information. Regulations regarding privacy were not as strict. The potential of personalized experiences, driven by vast datasets, seemed almost limitless. Brands, irrespective of their size and domain, reveled in this age of information, harnessing it to drive engagement, sales, and customer loyalty. However, this free reign was not without its repercussions, leading to breaches of privacy, compromised data, and a growing distrust among users.

Cambridge Analytica

A notable example of a major privacy breach was by the British consulting firm, Cambridge Analytica. Facebook's poor data privacy practices meant the app accessed the data of 87 million Facebook users without their consent. This data was then used to target political advertisements ahead of the 2016 US presidential elections. When this came to light in 2018, it led to a severe outcry, particularly in the European Union. Thus, the stage was set for the Internet's first data sheriff: GDPR.

(continued)

The Old Regime: Flexibility at a Cost

Before the introduction of GDPR, data collection policies were, at best, a patchwork of company-specific protocols, some stringent, others notably lax. This inconsistency, while offering businesses flexibility, created an environment where user data could easily fall through the cracks, leading to misuse and breaches.

GDPR's Entrance: A Regulatory Vanguard

In 2018, GDPR ushered in a new chapter, setting out strict guidelines for how organizations must handle, process, and store personal data. This regulation was a wake-up call for businesses that previously operated in an environment where data accessibility was unrestricted. Older systems, designed before these regulations, suddenly became potential problems.

While GDPR compliance was non-negotiable, how businesses approached this mandate varied. Newer startups, like Slack and Airbnb, were quick to adapt, building their data systems with GDPR in mind from the start. In contrast, established giants like Facebook and Google faced a more arduous journey, needing to upgrade their old systems to meet the new standards.

Lessons from the GDPR Transition

The shift toward GDPR illuminated broader industry lessons about preparedness, agility, and user trust. While legacy systems and expansive datasets were once seen as assets, they now carry the weight of compliance risks. But beyond mere compliance, GDPR underscored a fundamental business tenet: user trust is invaluable. Organizations that viewed GDPR not as a regulatory hurdle but as an opportunity to rebuild user trust found themselves better positioned in the new landscape.

(*continued*)

The GDPR narrative, much like Microsoft's transition to modern cloud services, highlights the challenges and opportunities that come with industry evolution. Just as Microsoft had to shift from traditional software to cloud-based solutions, businesses must adapt to new data privacy regulations. This evolution requires meeting regulatory and market standards and maintaining user trust and loyalty. Both journeys illustrate the importance of agility and proactive adaptation in a constantly changing landscape.

Audience Shift

AUDIENCE SHIFT

Evolving user needs, behaviors and preferences over time

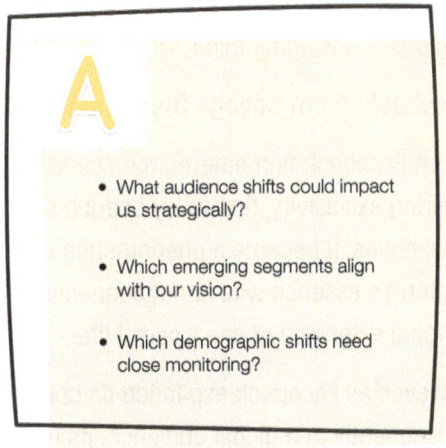

- What audience shifts could impact us strategically?

- Which emerging segments align with our vision?

- Which demographic shifts need close monitoring?

Designing for a shifting audience means constantly updating the user experience to align with changing preferences. This keeps the product relevant, ensuring sustained engagement and attracting new user segments, thereby preserving and potentially increasing revenue streams.

Questions to ask:

- What audience shifts could impact us strategically?

- Which emerging segments align with our vision?

- Which demographic shifts need close monitoring?

Audience Shift in Social Media: Facebook's Journey and the Rise of New Entrants

In the history of the Internet, few platforms have had as significant an impact as Facebook. Its continued relevance today—albeit to a different audience than its inception—is due to its ability to adapt to shifting audiences. I remember my college days fondly when Facebook was just starting to gain popularity. Only a select few campuses, including mine, were granted access to the new social platform.

Facebook: From College Dorms to Global Dominance

When Facebook first entered the scene, its target was clear: college students. Offering exclusivity, first to Ivy League schools and then gradually to other universities, it became a phenomenon among young adults and Millennials. The platform's essence was about connecting friends, sharing experiences, and creating a digital extension of one's social life.

However, as Facebook expanded its horizons, opening to the general public and subsequently to a global audience, its user base diversified. What was once a platform for the youth saw an influx of older generations.

(continued)

The Generational Drift: Boomers, Gen X, Millennials, and Gen Z

Once Facebook opened to the public, younger generations began to drop off as parents, grandparents, and extended families began flooding into the network. As soon as my mom joined Facebook, I was out. Younger users began to feel the platform was no longer the exclusive domain it once was. The presence of older family members, combined with Facebook's evolving algorithm and commercialization, as well as its politicization, diluted its appeal.

For Gen X, sandwiched between the Boomers and Millennials, the shift was more nuanced. Many of them adopted Facebook as a bridge—connecting with old school friends and family while also engaging with younger users. Yet, as platforms continued to evolve, portions of Gen X gravitated toward X (formerly known as Twitter) for its concise, real-time discourse and Instagram for visual storytelling.

As a Millennial, I looked for new digital hangouts, with platforms like Instagram and Twitter becoming go-to alternatives. But the real disruptor to Facebook has been TikTok. Providing short, engaging video content, it spoke the language of a younger generation, particularly Gen Z. Discord, originally a platform for gamers, also became popular among Gen Z, offering interactive spaces and online communities, like what AOL Instant Messenger (AIM) did in the early 2000s for my generation. Like AIM, Discord provides a sense of belonging, which resonates with a generation looking for deeper, more interactive social experiences.

(*continued*)

Strategic Implications of Audience Shift

Facebook's trajectory and the rise of alternative platforms underscore vital strategic lessons:

- Adaptation is Key: Platforms must evolve with their audience. While expansion is essential, platforms must ensure they retain the essence that made them appealing in the first place.

- Diversification vs. Specialization: While Facebook diversified, platforms like Instagram, Twitter, and TikTok found success in specializing and catering to specific audience needs.

Understanding Generational Needs: Each generation interacts with technology differently. Boomers may seek connection and nostalgia, Gen X bridges the digital gap between analog and digital, Millennials prioritize storytelling and aesthetics, Gen Z thrives on spontaneity and virality, and Gen Alpha idolizes Internet celebrities and kinetic content.

Mapping the Future: Navigating Audience Dynamics

As the audience shifts, so do platform priorities. Facebook, recognizing the drift, made strategic acquisitions like Instagram and WhatsApp, ensuring they have a foothold among diverse age groups. Meanwhile, newer platforms continually innovate, ensuring they remain relevant in a rapidly changing digital landscape.

The story of Facebook, alongside the rise of newer platforms, highlights the importance of monitoring and responding quickly to audience shifts. Not every company can pivot quickly—even Facebook struggled with its last big pivot, which led them to its latest rebrand as Meta. But from the numbers, their rebrand is starting to pay off.

Competition

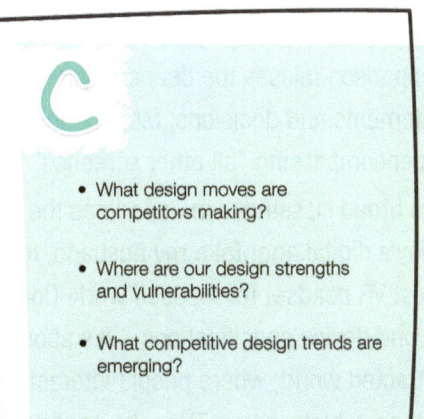

COMPETITION

Impact of rival companies on
design strategy

- What design moves are
  competitors making?

- Where are our design strengths
  and vulnerabilities?

- What competitive design trends are
  emerging?

Staying ahead or at least on par with competitors is key to revenue
protection and growth. Strategically differentiating products in design
can command premium pricing, increase market share, and drive user
acquisition, all contributing to increased revenues.

Questions to ask:

- What design moves are competitors making?

- Where are our design strengths and vulnerabilities?

- What competitive design trends are emerging?

Beyond Direct Rivals: Meta's Perspective

On the surface, it might seem logical to pit Meta's Quest headsets against direct tech competitors like Apple's Vision Pro. However, this direct product-to-product comparison misses the deeper layers of Meta's strategic outlook. Rooted in its statements and decisions, Meta defines its competition not just as similar products but encompassing "all other screens."

This broad classification underlines the changing dimensions of competition in today's digital age. Take my husband, for example, who regularly uses the Meta Quest VR headset for focused work. Competition for his time and attention goes beyond device specifications—it's about what he's trying to achieve. And in our distracted world, where people interact with multiple screens daily—smartphones, laptops, tablets, smart TVs—he needs focus. The VR headset helps him stay on task in a way other screens can't, showing how Meta has made moves to capture and retain user attention in innovative ways.

A few implications arise from this broader perspective:

- Understanding User Interactions: Instead of solely focusing on direct product features, there's a need to understand the myriad of digital interactions that punctuate a user's day. The goal is to identify gaps and opportunities to make the experience more compelling than others.

- Elevating User Experience: Price and features are important but the overall user experience—ranging from interface design to software integration—must also be considered. A product might be competitively priced but if its user experience is subpar, retention becomes a challenge.

- Holistic Engagement: The emphasis shifts from simply marketing a product's features to engaging users in a more complete and meaningful way. This means understanding their online habits, preferences, and challenges, and providing solutions that fit easily into their lives.

The main point for businesses is simple: In a world overflowing with distraction, companies are not only competing with direct rivals but also with every interaction that captures a person's attention.

Economic Trends

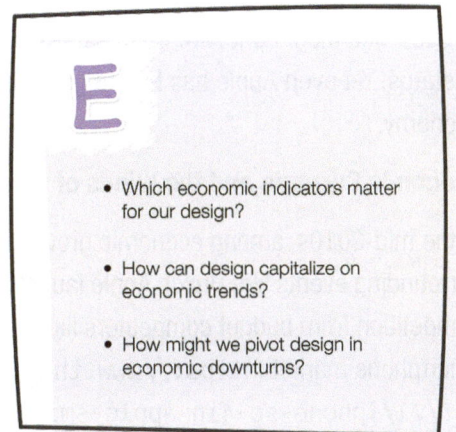

ECONOMIC
TRENDS

Broader financial decisions
influencing design choices

Economic shifts influence consumer spending and product affordability. Strategists must recognize these fluctuations to align products with users' financial realities. By integrating these insights, businesses can optimize product positioning, ensuring consistent revenue even during economic downturns.

Questions to ask:

- Which economic indicators matter for our design?

- How can design capitalize on economic trends?

- How might we pivot design in economic downturns?

Strategic Positioning in a Shifting Economic Landscape: Apple's iPhone SE

For much of its history, Apple has been known for creating high-end products. Its devices, like the iPhone, are impressive technologies that also function as symbols of status. Yet even Apple has had to grapple with the realities of a volatile global economy.

Economic Currents and the Winds of Change

In the mid-2010s, among economic growth concerns and political uncertainties surrounding events like Brexit, Apple launched the iPhone SE in response to competition from budget competitors like Samsung, Huawei, and Xiaomi in a crowded smartphone market (https://www.theguardian.com/technology/2016/mar/21/iphone-se-4in-apple-smartphone-launched-cheaper-price). These companies presented reasonably priced smartphones with features posing a threat to Apple's dominance in the market. The SE was Apple's response to these pressures—a more affordable model aimed at attracting budget-conscious consumers.

The iPhone SE Gambit

In a move that surprised many, Apple introduced the iPhone SE—it's lowest priced phone. With a price tag much lower than its flagship siblings, the SE stood out because it offered a premium experience without the premium price. This made it very appealing, especially in emerging markets where middle-class consumers wanted a taste of luxury.

But this wasn't just a reaction to competition. Apple's introduction of the SE was a smart, strategic move. They weren't just responding to pressures; they were anticipating a shift. The goal? To provide value without losing what makes an iPhone special.

(continued)

Dilemmas of Brand Identity and the Road Ahead

Launching a product like the iPhone SE was not without risk. There was the potential of diluting Apple's hard-earned brand image, of making the iPhone commonplace. Yet, with strategic finesse, Apple ensured the SE was perceived not as a "cheaper iPhone" but as an "iPhone for everyone."

The continued iterations and success of the SE line underscore a larger truth: Companies, no matter their stature, must be prepared to adapt to changing circumstances and respond to broader economic trends when necessary by integrating these insights into their decision-making frameworks.

Substitute Technologies

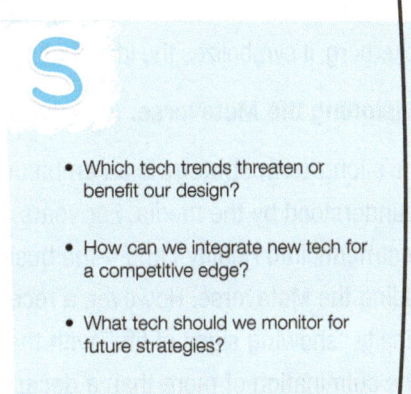

SUBSTITUTE
TECHNOLOGIES

Emerging tech that could
replace the current design

S

- Which tech trends threaten or benefit our design?

- How can we integrate new tech for a competitive edge?

- What tech should we monitor for future strategies?

Embracing emerging technologies can tap into new revenue streams and position a company as an industry innovator. Users value impactful and useful features. What is considered "useful" changes with time, and neglecting these trends risks obsolescence, user attrition, and revenue decline. Thinking proactively ensures a clearer understanding of what technologies are required to remain relevant and competitive.

Questions to ask:

- Which tech trends threaten or benefit our design?

- How can we integrate new tech for a competitive edge?

- What tech should we monitor for future strategies?

Facebook to Meta: An Internal Disruption in Pursuit of Future-Proofing

When Facebook debuted in 2004, it tapped into a hunger for digital connection. The company emerged as a social media giant, with the platform quickly becoming a fixture in our daily lives. However, technology did not stop evolving and neither did Facebook's aspirations.

Recognizing that standing still means falling behind, Facebook made a daring move: It disrupted itself. Not just in name but in vision and mission. Enter Meta. In Greek, it means "after" or "beyond," but it can also mean "with" or "alongside." This aspect speaks to the creation of a metaverse—a reality that exists alongside our own. According to Mark Zuckerberg, it symbolizes the idea that "There's always more to build."[1]

Envisioning the Metaverse: A Paradigm Shift

Meta's long-term strategy is an ambitious one, and one that has often been misunderstood by the media. For years, they've reported on Meta's "wasted" investments into Reality Labs—the business and research unit responsible for building the Metaverse. However, a recent report from MSNBC highlights that Meta is finally "showing signs of life" with the showcase of the Orion smart glasses. It is the culmination of more than a decade of investment into virtual reality (VR) and augmented reality (AR) technology (collectively "XR") and is just a glimpse into the progress they've made so far.

(continued)

---

[1] Smith, Adam, "What Does Facebook's New Name 'Meta' and 'Metaverse' Mean?" The Independent, 29 Oct. 2021, www.independent.co.uk/tech/facebook-meta-metaverse-rename-meaning-b1947654.html.

During the pandemic, I had first-hand experience with a headset produced by Meta's Reality Labs. Going from country to country and quarantine to quarantine, I was able to use a Meta Quest 2 VR headset to see friends and family in a way that felt infinitely more tangible and immediate than a Zoom or Facetime call. This was just a few years ago and I could already see the direction that Meta was going.

Products like the Meta Quest VR headsets and Orion AR smart glasses offer a glimpse of a future where digital interaction goes beyond passive scrolling and becomes an active, immersive, and emotional experience.

The Cost of Transformation: Internal Realignments

To make the Metaverse vision a reality, Meta underwent a huge internal pivot. Originally a social media giant, they weren't experts in hardware. This meant not only realigning goals but also talent. A significant number of employees, once crucial in Facebook's rise, found their skills misaligned with the needs of Meta's metaverse objectives. Consequently, the company faced tough decisions, resulting in layoffs. Transitioning from a primarily software-centric entity to one integrating cutting-edge hardware, software, and experiential design required fresh expertise and a shift in company culture.

Preparing for a New Digital Age: A Generational Pivot

Meta's focus isn't just about current technologies; it's about anticipating and meeting the demands of future XR natives. For incoming generations, distinctions between AR, VR, and traditional screen-based interactions will blur, and Meta aims to create tools and platforms that speak to their future user base. These tools and platforms are funded by Facebook's legacy successes. This has enabled the company to take a much bigger risk in newer domains because it has the financial foundation to sustain ongoing operations while also supporting experiments in innovation.

Understanding Alignment and Responding to Change

I have a close friend who is 5'9 while I'm 5'1. She jokes that we're like Pinky and the Brain. Once we were attending a conference together, and she disappeared. I tried to get ahold of her but couldn't, which had me worried. Eventually when I reached her, she explained to me she smacked her head on the bottom of a staircase with a low clearance and it had caused a small cut above her hairline. She had gone to the bathroom to tend to her injury. Had I walked through the same area, nothing would have happened. Because I'm height-challenged, spaces with low clearances are simply not a threat to me.

This situation made me think about how businesses need to categorize their risks. Just like the low clearance of the staircase posed a danger to my friend but was harmless for me, some risks may be critical for one business but irrelevant for another. Understanding which risks are material to your operation is key. What might seem like a minor issue to one company could be catastrophic for another. Just as we can't all dodge the same obstacles, businesses need to assess what poses a real threat and prioritize mitigating those risks.

Incorporating the TRACES framework into your strategic approach empowers you as a design leader in several key ways. By aligning the team around shared definitions of threats such as Technical Debt, Regulatory Changes, Audience Shift, Competition, Economic Trends, and Substitute Technologies, you can create a common understanding that allows your team to prioritize issues effectively and address the most pressing challenges together.

TRACES provides a clear rationale for your strategies, aligns design initiatives with overall business objectives, and underscores the critical role of design in navigating the company through a constantly evolving, complex business landscape. This approach positions the design function as a key strategic partner in the organization's success.

Facilitating Insightful Dialogues on Strategic Response

- Understanding Alignment and Responding to Change

  - Assessing Alignment: Evaluate how well your current design objectives align with broader company goals. This helps ensure your design initiatives contribute meaningfully to the organization's success.

  - Monitoring TRACES: Once alignment is established, turn your attention to the TRACES elements. These represent the dynamic external factors that can significantly impact your strategic direction.

- Making Strategic Adjustments with TRACES

  - Interpreting Signals from TRACES: Each element of TRACES provides signals about the external environment that can influence your design strategy. For example: A shift in audience preferences might indicate the need for a design adjustment. Emerging substitute technologies could offer new opportunities for innovation. Economic trends might necessitate a more cost-efficient design approach.

  - Adapting to External Changes: As external factors shift, your design strategy should adapt accordingly. This adaptation might mean moving from optimization to transformation if new technologies disrupt your industry. It could also mean enhancing processes to comply with new regulations or adapting team structures in response to competitive pressures.

- Balancing Internal and External Dynamics

  - Internal Environment: While focusing on internal efficiency and optimization, consider how external changes might necessitate a pivot in your approach. Your internal environment should be flexible enough to accommodate necessary strategic shifts.

  - External Environment: Keep a pulse on the external environment through TRACES. It will guide you in making informed decisions about when to enhance, adapt, or transform your design strategies.

  - Continuous Reassessment: Regularly review your internal alignment and your risks. This ongoing process ensures that your design strategy responds to current needs and is agile enough to adapt to future changes.

Practical Application: Threat Identification Canvas

The Threat Identification Canvas prompts design leaders to list major threats in each TRACES category. Example threats might include the emergence of AI-powered competitive product alternatives, disruptions to critical supply chains, rapid shifts in user preferences, evolving privacy or environmental policy regulations requiring compliance, etcetera. By mapping threats across these key categories, design leaders can build a more robust understanding of the various risks that should be monitored and managed.

Key Benefits of the Canvas:

- Prevents Costly Oversights:

  Addressing vulnerabilities early in the design cycle is significantly more cost-effective than dealing with them during product launch or maintenance. Remediation of late-stage oversights often results in schedule delays, solution reworks, and significant cost overages. Early identification and management of threats prevent them from escalating into serious issues that require expensive and extensive corrections.

- Enhances Adaptability and Resilience:

  By evaluating a range of scenarios from identified threats, teams can develop strategies to respond effectively to turbulent events. This readiness means rapidly adapting to unexpected customer shifts, supply chain disruptions, competitive threats, and other destabilizing external changes.

- Fosters Collaboration and Communication:

  The collaborative process of risk identification fosters teamwork and ensures that all team members have a common understanding of potential risks. This shared perspective is crucial for effective risk management and strategic planning.

Threat Identification Canvas

The Threat Identification Canvas (Figure 3-2) is a tool to systematically identify threats across key areas that could undermine a product or service's ability to reliably deliver customer benefits.

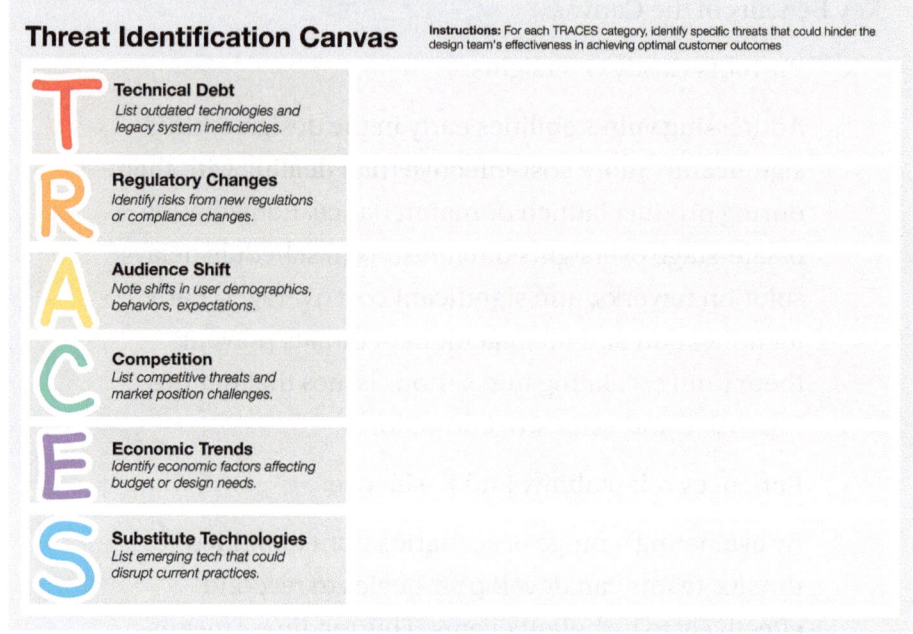

Figure 3-2. *Threat Identification Canvas*

Components of the Threat Identification Canvas

The canvas provides a template for collaborative brainstorming workshops to identify threats across six categories:

- Technical Debt (T)—Infrastructure vulnerabilities, legacy tech debt, system dependencies

- Regulatory Changes (R)—Policy, legal, compliance, audit, standards risks

- Audience Shift (A)—User preferences, demographic changes, retention risks

- Competition (C)—Market rivals, new entrants, alternative offerings

- Economic Trends (E)—Macrofinancial trends, regional risks, budgets

- Substitute Technologies (S)—Emerging displacements, paradigm shifts

Workshop Introduction: Identifying Threats with the TRACES Framework

Our first step is gaining clarity on threats we currently face across technical, regulatory, audience, competitive, economic, and substitution dimensions (i.e., TRACES). How well do we understand our risk landscape? Have we overlooked blind spots? Identifying vulnerabilities early allows us to mitigate risks proactively.

The Role of the Canvas

We'll use the Threat Identification Canvas to methodically map risks in each TRACES area, prompting discussions to uncover overt and latent threats. The canvas builds collective intelligence on hazards that threaten to undermine the delivery of value and service to our customers.

Workshop Objectives

- Evaluate Exposure: Assess known and potential threats in our business environment

- Discover Blind Spots: Uncover overlooked or underappreciated risks

- Inform Resilience Plans: Develop risk-based strategies for adaptability

Participant Selection

The ideal participant group size is between 8 and 12. This session will focus on identifying threats. Table 3-1 lists the participants that should be included. The same participants from this initial risk identification session should be invited to the follow-up workshop (detailed in the next chapter), particularly the same subject matter experts who highlighted the risks.

Table 3-1. *Ideal participant list*

Department	Roles
Senior Management	Chief Operating Officer (COO)
Governance/Compliance	Compliance Manager
Finance and Risk	Risk Manager
Legal	Legal Counsel
Human Resources	HR Manager
IT	IT Security Officer IT Manager Development Manager
Design	Chief Design Officer (CDO) User Research Lead Design Manager
Marketing	Marketing Manager Customer Experience Lead Analytics Lead
Others (Optional)	Chief Customer Officer Chief Analytics Officer Data/Business Intelligence Analysts Customer service/support reps

Preparing for the Workshop

- Materials Preparation: Print 1 A1 size Threat Identification Canvas for group activity, Post-Its, sharpies.

- Logistics Setup: Arrange space, post canvas templates around the room.

Table 3-2 provides a template for the workshop's agenda.

Table 3-2. *Workshop agenda*

	Rundown		Time
09:30–09:45	Introduction	Overview of threat scanning goals and TRACES categories	15 mins
09:45–9:50	Canvas Tool Briefing	Explain use of canvas to map threats during session	5 mins
09:50–10:50	Group Mapping Activity	Group works together to populate canvas with identified threats	60 mins
10:50–11:20	Group Presentation	Facilitate group discussion on whether the alignment is desirable and strategically beneficial.	30 mins
11:20–11:30	Conclusion	Recap key insights and next step actions	10 mins

After the Workshop

- Email Summary: Share post-workshop summary and document threats discussed.

- Schedule a Follow-Up: Schedule risk mitigation strategy workshop with the same cross-functional group.

- Continuous Review: Regularly provide updates as threats evolve or new ones emerge.

The objective of this first working session is to bring together subject matter experts and leaders from diverse functions—spanning technology, design, legal, finance, and more—to leverage their unique perspectives in assessing and defining the top risks facing the organization.

Guided by the six risk categories in the Threat Identification Canvas centered on technical debt, regulations, audience shifts, competition, economics, and substitution, participants will collaborate to surface, discuss, and prioritize the threats they view as most impactful if left unmanaged.

The desired output is a collective perspective on the current highest priority risk exposures identified across the operational dimensions covered by the cross-functional team. This will set the foundation to then converge on risk mitigation strategies in a follow-up workshop.

Key Takeaways

- The TRACES framework stands for Technical debt, Regulatory changes, Audience shift, Competition, Economic trends, and Substitute technologies.

- TRACES helps adapt design strategies in response to shifts in external factors.

- The Threat Identification Canvas, coupled with the TRACES framework, allows design leaders to systematically identify potential threats.

CHAPTER 4

Strategic Adaptation and Risk Management in Design

Now it's time to make decisions about which threats to tackle first—considering how likely they are to occur and how badly it'll hurt if not dealt with quickly. We'll use the Adaptive Risk Response (ARR) Model, a framework that builds on traditional risk matrices by adding a time dimension. We don't always have the time or the resources to address all threats at once, so the ARR model helps design leaders prioritize. The risk model provides a visualization of how resources could be allocated to address immediate risks and build resilience for the future. This allows designers to proactively shape creative solutions, rather than simply reacting to the problems of the present.

In this chapter, you will learn how to

- Apply the Adaptive Risk Response (ARR) Model

- Assess and categorize threats based on their likelihood and urgency

- Allocate resources to address risks most relevant at that moment

© Garkay Wong 2025
G. Wong, *The Art of Design Strategy*, Design Thinking,
https://doi.org/10.1007/979-8-8688-0552-3_4

Closing the Gap

In 2001, Gap Inc. was the largest specialty retailer in the United States. As a brand, it redefined American casual wear, turning the simple jeans-and-T-shirt look into a fashion statement. Gap wasn't just a brand; it was a cultural icon, the tacitly agreed-upon "uniform" for nearly every American. Its catchy marketing campaigns featuring popular American celebrities like Ryan Adams, Willie Nelson, Joan Didion, and others, only cemented what we already knew: the "Gap look" is "default American."

However, the late 2000s and early 2010s saw a shift in economic conditions that notably impacted consumer spending habits. This period amplified risks for apparel retailers, including Gap. As a result of continued economic trends and tightened consumer budgets, in 2019 Gap reported a 4% year-over-year decrease in comparable sales across all of its brands, with the Gap brand experiencing the steepest decline at 7%.[1] These figures reflected the challenges posed by changing consumer preferences and economic uncertainties.

The emergence of fast fashion competitors like Zara and H&M, as well as the rise of e-commerce didn't help matters. As financial pressure began to mount, it became difficult to maintain market share. Internally, Gap was slow to adapt to e-commerce to compete against direct-to-consumer brands. Consumers' growing preference for online shopping marked a significant departure from traditional mall-based retail.

Over the years, consumers increasingly opted for the convenience of online shopping, and Gap was forced to confront its technological debt. Outdated IT systems and digital infrastructure hindered the company's ability to adapt swiftly to the new digital retail landscape.

---

[1] Biron, Bethany, "The Rise and Fall of Gap, One of the Most Iconic and Beloved American Retailers," Business Insider, 13 Nov. 2019, www.businessinsider.in/retail/news/the-rise-and-fall-of-gap-one-of-the-most-iconic-and-beloved-american-retailers/articleshow/72030634.cms.

Competing mobile shopping apps and online fashion platforms were disrupting the retail industry by introducing new experiences that offered convenience and flexibility through mobile-enabled purchase and delivery of goods. These platforms also provided a broader range of styles and options than would be available in a physical store. This increase in agility enabled rivals to outpace Gap, which had a slower integration of technology. Not only did Gap have the challenge of overhauling its brand's digital presence, it also had to integrate new technologies to meet evolving consumer expectations in an industry increasingly defined by speed, convenience, and responsiveness to trends.

Gap has become a cautionary tale within the retail industry. Gap's story highlights the risks of not moving fast enough to keep pace with changing consumer demands. Gap's struggle to regain its dominant position after failing to address emerging threats underscores the need for proactive and timely risk mitigation strategies to ensure that opportunities are not missed when dealing with a more diverse and technology-oriented customer base.[2]

Quick Tests, Not Quick Wins

 Kevin Tong is a Lead Product Designer at BCG Digital Ventures. During his time there, he built startups for some of the world's most impactful organizations across a wide range of industries, including financial services, healthcare, fashion, agriculture, and retail. He's committed to pushing design beyond aesthetics and into strategy, collaboration, and ethical impact.

(continued)

---

[2] "Gap Inc. Reports Fourth Quarter and Fiscal 2022 Results," Gap Inc, 9 Mar. 2023, https://www.gapinc.com/en-us/articles/2023/03/gap-inc-reports-fourth-quarter-and-fiscal-2022-res.

Quick Tests, Not Quick Wins

When building game-changing ventures, the focus should be to uncover the fundamental "why" behind a product or service. This approach is crucial for new-stage ventures and established products, each presenting its own challenges and lessons.

From the perspective of a new-stage venture, corporate visions often originate as grand plans crafted by executives. These strategies might align perfectly with the company's mission and seem flawless on paper. However, they frequently fall short in the real world, despite substantial investments of time, effort, money, and resources. The critical takeaway is the necessity of testing the riskiest assumptions at the conceptual stage.

I worked on a venture in Southeast Asia where the initial brief was to launch a health-focused super app—essentially a "WeChat for health." By testing the core hypothesis early on, we shifted to a leaner Minimum Viable Product (MVP) that resonated more effectively with users. This pivot led to a launch product that has since garnered over four million users and become a beloved service in the region.

From the perspective of an established product, a common pattern is the obsession with quick wins. While tempting due to the lower effort and perceived safety in decision-making, this approach often results in a series of band-aid solutions. These quick fixes accumulate, leading to a product that lacks quality and offers a disjointed user experience. Focusing solely on quick wins might improve how someone uses a product but neglects the crucial understanding of why they use it.

A case in point was an Australian company that dominated its industry for nearly 20 years. They started with an MVP but never evolved beyond that mindset, continuously adding quick fixes without a cohesive vision. The result was a fragmented product experience that suffered in quality and usability. By realigning with the original vision and testing it with customers, we streamlined the product, enhancing the user experience and providing a renewed focus for the company.

(continued)

Quick Tests, Not Quick Wins

It's essential to test assumptions at all stages of a product's life cycle and maintain a steadfast focus on the "why." In the early stages, this means reducing risk to uncover the core purpose of the product. In later stages, it involves ensuring product quality and alignment with the overarching vision. A company must cultivate a culture of transparency, embrace failure as a learning opportunity, and commit to continuous improvement.

—Kevin Tong

Adapting to Emerging Risks with Agility

Early in my career, I was working at a startup on a product designed to help pet owners keep track of their furry companions. We decided to use low-cost beacon technology to triangulate pets' locations, which felt like a groundbreaking solution at the time. I can still remember the excitement as we prepared to showcase our app at SuperZoo, one of the biggest pet industry events. Back then, GPS pet trackers were prohibitively expensive, with hefty subscription fees. This made our beacon-based solution stand out as affordable and innovative. We built the app on top of this technology, feeling confident that we were solving a real problem for pet owners.

But tech never stands still. Over time, customer attitudes shifted as GPS technology became more accessible, affordable, and available from a growing number of competitors. The market's expectations changed, and suddenly, what we once saw as our advantage—beacon technology— became a hindrance. Customers now saw GPS as the baseline and our once-innovative solution started to look outdated.

Had we understood how fast the technology was evolving and considered customer demands, we could have begun transitioning to GPS earlier. But by the time we realized the issue, it was too late. Our initial technology had become a barrier, and eventually, the business couldn't sustain itself.

Traditional risk matrices evaluate risks by assessing their probability and impact, serving as a basic method for risk assessment. However, without considering the time dimension it can be difficult to prioritize effectively. How do we prioritize risks that don't pose an immediate threat? With the pet app, we didn't consider the possibility that GPS technology would eventually be so commonplace that it would be included in every phone and every vehicle. It wasn't an immediate threat and, therefore, it wasn't in our risk matrices.

If design is always reacting to current risks, it will always be playing catch-up and run the risk of creating products or experiences that are no longer relevant by the time they are ready for launch.

This model helps design teams get ahead of these risks by categorizing threats into time horizons and assessing their probability and impact. By adopting a more dynamic approach, design leaders can adjust their risk mitigation strategies as conditions and priorities change.

The threats identified in the previous chapter are plotted on a framework that evaluates risks across two main dimensions: Impact Probability and Time to Materialization.

- Impact Probability (Likelihood): This axis (Table 4-1) gauges the likelihood of a threat or challenge impacting the organization, especially in terms of affecting the design function and its ability to deliver customer-centric outcomes.

  - High Impact Probability: Indicates a threat is very likely to affect the design team's output and customer satisfaction significantly. You cannot afford to ignore these issues.

  - Moderate Impact Probability: These threats might affect the team or outcomes, but the impact is not as immediate or severe. They require a balanced approach.

- Minimal Impact Probability: Low-probability threats
  that might have only a slight or indirect effect on the
  design team's effectiveness or service outcomes.

Table 4-1. *Impact severity definitions*

Impact Severity Definitions

	Low Impact	Medium Impact	High Impact
Technical Debt	Minor legacy issues; no immediate impact	Some outdated systems affect performance but will not impede long-term goals.	Significant technical debt that not only jeopardizes immediate efficiency but also hinders long-term innovation.
Regulatory Changes	Design complies with current regulations	Some anticipated changes may need minor adjustments	Upcoming regulations require significant design overhaul
Audience Shift	Stable user base; minor preference changes	Emerging user segments; evolving needs	Rapid shifts in audience behavior or demographics
Competition	Dominant market position; few challengers	Notable competitors emerging; minor market share loss	Strong competitors pose significant threat to market position
Economic Trends	Stable economic conditions; minimal impact	Some economic shifts; minor design implications	Major economic trends necessitating design strategy revamp
Substitute Technologies	Sticking with industry-standard tech	Noticing emerging tech trends; potential relevance	Rapid adoption of new tech, altering design practices

- Time to Materialization (Urgency): This axis indicates the time frame within which a potential threat or challenge is expected to become a reality (Figure 4-1).

- Short Term (up to 1 year): Looming threats or those anticipated to emerge within the upcoming year require readiness or immediate action. A tactical and reactive approach is essential in this context.

- Medium Term (1–3 years): While not immediate, these threats are anticipated to materialize in the medium term. This time frame allows for more strategic planning and proactive measures.

- Long Term (beyond 3 years): Long-range threats that give you ample time to plan, monitor, and adapt strategies for future scenarios.

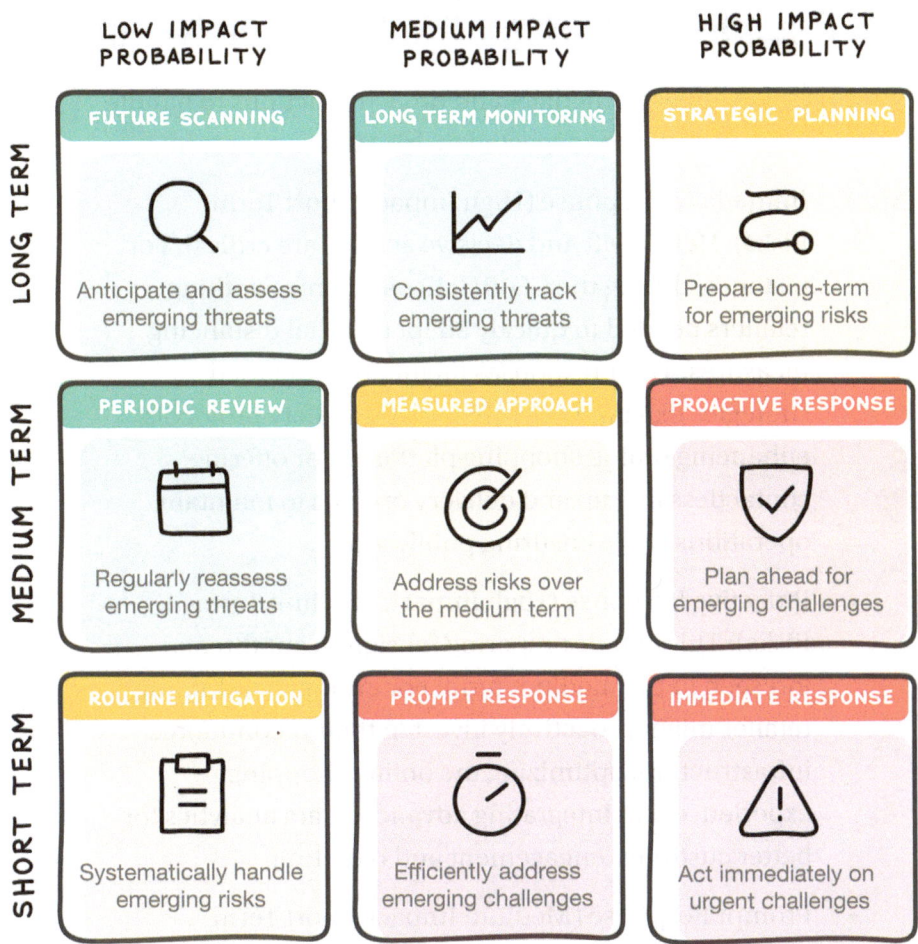

Figure 4-1. *Adaptive Risk Response (ARR) Model*

The ARR Model divides threat management into three distinct zones, each focusing on varying aspects of response and urgency.

Risk Response Strategy (Red): Action Needed

The Red zone involves immediate and proactive actions to handle imminent threats or threats expected to arise in the near term.

- Immediate Response (High Impact, Short Term Risks): Here, swift and decisive actions are critical. For instance, during the COVID-19 pandemic, clothing retailers needed to quickly adapt to social distancing measures. Their responses might have included strategies like implementing in-store safety protocols, enhancing online shopping platforms, or offering contactless pickup and delivery options to maintain operations while ensuring public safety.

- Proactive Response (High Impact, Medium Term Risks): This entails preparing for significant threats foreseen in the medium term. For example, a clothing retailer might proactively invest in their e-commerce infrastructure, optimizing the online shopping experience and integrating advanced data analytics for better customer engagement and retention.

- Prompt Response (Medium Impact, Short Term Risks): This involves efficiently tackling moderate-impact, imminent threats. For example, if a clothing retailer notices a trend toward casual and comfortable clothing, it can swiftly adjust its inventory to include more loungewear and athleisure, responding efficiently to the changing customer preferences.

Risk Mitigation Strategy (Yellow): Planning Needed

The Yellow band focuses on strategic planning and balanced approaches to manage medium-term risks and prepare for high-impact long-term threats.

- Strategic Planning (High Impact, Long Term Risks): This entails developing comprehensive, long-term strategies for major risks, incorporating them into the broader organizational vision. For example, a retailer might recognize the potential long-term shift toward ethical and sustainable fashion and embark on a comprehensive strategy to overhaul their brand identity to align with these values. This could include long-term investments in sustainable supply chains, partnerships with eco-conscious designers, and marketing campaigns to reposition the brand in the market.

- Measured Approach (Medium Impact, Medium Term Risks): This strategy balances resource allocation and planning for moderate risks expected to manifest in the medium term. For example, a clothing retailer might introduce a sustainability initiative in response to growing environmental concerns. This could involve a gradual shift toward sourcing eco-friendly materials and implementing ethical manufacturing processes.

- Routine Mitigation (Low Impact, Short Term Risks): This involves managing emerging threats of low impact with consistent, ongoing efforts. For example, a clothing retailer might implement a dynamic inventory management system to proactively address evolving fashion trends and consumer preferences.

Risk Monitoring Strategy (Green): Oversight Needed

The Green zone is about ongoing oversight and future-focused planning to manage less critical but potentially evolving threats.

- Long-Term Monitoring (Medium Impact, Long-Term Risks): This strategy focuses on the continuous observation and tracking of moderate risks anticipated in the distant future. A cloud services provider might invest in industry research to continuously monitor trends in energy costs and consumption. By having robust monitoring, the cloud services provider can anticipate and prepare for future shifts in the source and costs of energy.

- Periodic Review (Low Impact, Medium Term Risks): This involves the regular reassessment of low-impact threats, updating strategies as needed over time. The retailer might routinely evaluate their customer engagement strategies, ensuring they are effectively reaching their target audience. This could involve analyzing social media engagement, customer feedback, and sales data to continually refine their marketing and customer service approaches.

- Future Scanning (Low Impact, Long Term Risks): This approach is about anticipating and preparing for future scenarios, particularly long-term, low-impact risks. For example, a clothing retailer might actively explore the integration of emerging technologies, such as augmented reality and virtual reality within their retail strategy. This exploration doesn't necessarily translate into immediate sales increases but it's a strategic move to keep the brand at the forefront of retail innovation. By staying abreast of technological trends, the retailer is prepared to adopt new solutions as they become more viable and positions itself as a forward-thinking player in the market, ready to meet future consumer demands and expectations in a digital-first shopping landscape.

The ARR model enables a way to prioritize threats based on urgency and impact to the organization. Design strategies can be crafted around mitigating those specific risks. Additionally, regularly revisiting long-term risks can help determine whether previously identified threats still pose a significant risk. If not, resources from risks that didn't materialize or no longer require the same level of attention can be diverted to areas with more pressing issues or new threats.

Practical Application: The Adaptive Risk Response Canvas

The Adaptive Risk Response Canvas helps design teams think strategically and solve problems proactively. It organizes threats based on severity and timeline, making it easier for design leaders to make decisions around risks and their potential impact on the organization's customer service delivery. This flexibility offers an advantage over static response plans and enables design teams to proactively address emerging challenges rather than merely react to the disaster of the week.

The canvas can also serve as a valuable tool for design leaders to engage with senior leadership and stakeholders. It provides a clear record of the response strategies, including the reason for prioritizing specific tasks over others based on their urgency and potential impact. This documentation helps justify resource allocation decisions made in a given moment, relying on the best information available. This level of transparency helps stakeholders understand the rationale behind decisions, including how design initiatives link to strategic goals and timelines. As a result, upper management can put their trust and support behind the initiatives, knowing they are advancing their target outcomes.

Key Benefits:

- Structured Threat Management and Enhanced Preparedness: The canvas offers a structured framework for managing threats, categorizing them based on impact and urgency. It enables teams to develop targeted response, mitigation, and monitoring strategies for each threat category. This approach streamlines decision-making by prioritizing resources toward the most critical threats and enhances organizational preparedness for a range of scenarios.

- Facilitates Collaborative Strategy Development and Continuous Adaptation: Designed for collaborative sessions, the canvas encourages diverse perspectives in the planning of responses, leading to more robust strategies. It supports continuous review and strategic adaptation as threats evolve, keeping the organization's responses relevant and effective over time.

- Guides Strategic Planning and Long-Term Resilience: By including long-term planning for future threats, the canvas ensures that organizations are not merely reacting to immediate threats but are also proactively preparing for future challenges.

Adaptive Risk Response Canvas

The Adaptive Risk Response Canvas (Figure 4-2; Table 4-2) is a structured tool designed to facilitate the strategic management of identified threats, ensuring effective responses across areas of potential impact.

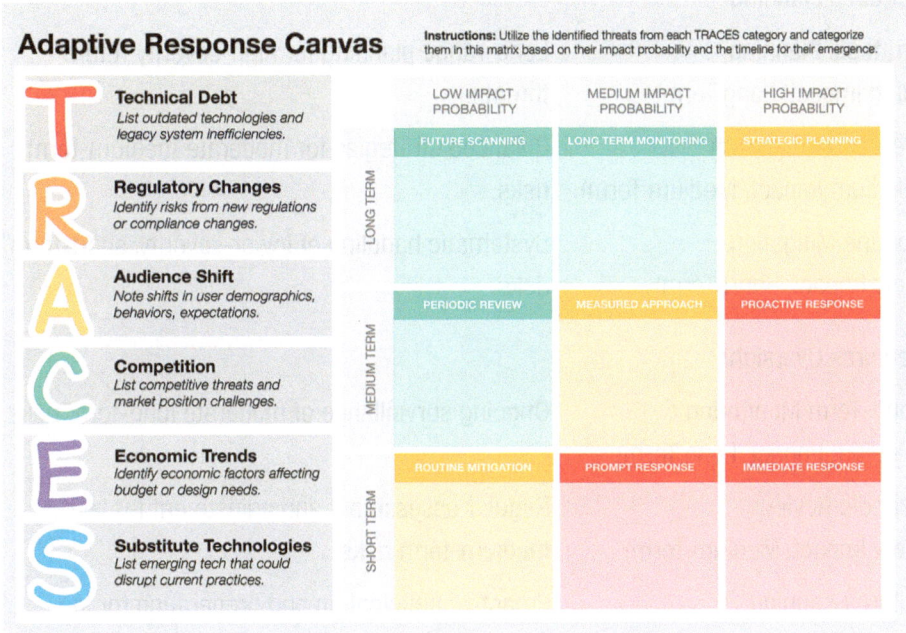

Figure 4-2. *Adaptive response canvas*

Table 4-2. *Components of the adaptive risk response canvas*

Threat Category	Description
Requires Action	
Immediate Response (High Impact, Short Term)	Urgent actions for imminent high-severity threats.
Proactive Response (High Impact, Medium Term)	Forward-planning for significant medium-term threats.
Prompt Response (Medium Impact, Short Term)	Timely reactions to moderately impactful threats.
Requires Planning	
Strategic Planning (High Impact, Long Term)	Long-range planning for high-severity future threats.
Measured Approach (Medium Impact, Medium Term)	Balanced strategies for moderate medium-term risks.
Routine Mitigation (Low Impact, Short Term)	Systematic handling of lower-severity, short-term risks.
Requires Oversight	
Long-Term Monitoring (Medium Impact, Long Term)	Ongoing surveillance of moderate long-term risks.
Periodic Review (Low Impact, Medium Term)	Regular assessment and adjustment for lesser medium-term risks.
Future Scanning (Low Impact, Long Term)	Proactive anticipation and preparation for low-severity long-term risks.

This canvas offers a template for collaborative sessions to strategize responses to threats in each category.

Workshop Introduction: Scenario Planning with the Adaptive Response Canvas

We'll revisit the threats we've previously identified using the TRACES Threat Identification Canvas. Our focus now shifts to strategizing our responses. For each threat, we'll consider its impact, immediacy, and the required action. Are we equipped to address these threats effectively?

The Role of the Canvas

The Adaptive Response Canvas will be our tool to systematically strategize our responses. This session aims to facilitate more pointed discussions that consider the severity and urgency of the identified threats. Timing matters—and by utilizing this strategic canvas, we can ensure that our efforts address the most critical and time-sensitive threats, while maintaining a view of emerging, longer term challenges.

Workshop Objectives

- Determine Response Strategies: Develop high-level plans for each threat based on its impact and expected timeline.

- Streamline Decision Making: Identify and prioritize resource allocation to address the most critical threats efficiently.

- Enhance Preparedness: Arm your team with a register of strategies to handle a range of threat scenarios effectively.

Participant Selection

This workshop should involve the same cross-functional group of 8–12 people that attended the TRACES Threat Identification workshop. The ideal list of participants to include is found in Table 4-3.

Table 4-3. *Participant list*

Department	Roles
Senior Management	Chief Operating Officer (COO)
Governance/Compliance	Compliance Manager
Finance and Risk	Risk Manager
Legal	Legal Counsel
Human Resources	HR Manager
IT	IT Security Officer IT Manager Development Manager
Design	Chief Design Officer (CDO) Chief Customer Officer User Research Lead Design Manager
Marketing	Marketing Manager Analytics Lead Customer Experience Lead
Others (Optional)	Chief Analytics Officer Data/Business Intelligence Analysts Customer service/support reps

Preparing for the Workshop

- Pre-Read Materials: Include reports about emerging trends (e.g., Gartner Hype Cycle) to help participants understand potential timelines and threats from an informed perspective.[3]

- Materials Preparation: Print 1 A1 Strategy Response Canvas to work on as a group. Include Post-Its and sharpies.

- Logistics Setup: Set up the workshop space to facilitate engagement and collaboration. Divide participants into small groups to encourage participation.

Table 4-4. *Agenda*

	Rundown		Time
09:30–09:45	Introduction	Outline the workshop's goals and the importance of the Strategic Response Canvas	15 mins
09:45–9:50	Canvas Tool Briefing	Guide participants on how to use the canvas	5 mins
09:50–10:20	Group Mapping Activity	Collaborative mapping of previously identified threats onto the canvas	30 mins
10:20–10:50	Response Strategy Development	Brainstorming session to create response, mitigation, and monitoring plans for each category	30 mins
10:50–11:00	Conclusion	Recap key insights and next step actions	10 mins

---

[3] Gartner, "Gartner Hype Cycle," www.gartner.com/en/research/methodologies/ gartner-hype-cycle, Accessed 3 Aug. 2024.

Post-Workshop Actions

- Email Summary: Share a report of the workshop and the strategic plans developed.

- Implementation Teams: Establish accountability for teams responsible for executing strategic responses or monitoring the threats.

- Continuous Review: Regularly update and adapt strategies as threats evolve or new ones emerge.

The scenario planning workshop helps teams develop actionable responses to key threats based on impact levels and expected timelines. Using the Adaptive Response Canvas, workshop participants map mitigation strategies to risks. This facilitates targeted preparations and optimizing resource allocations across functions. The collaborative process builds buy-in for execution of response strategies, thereby increasing organizational resilience.

Key Takeaways

- Gap's loss of market share illustrates the need for agility, foresight, and innovation in design strategy to remain competitive in fast-changing industries.

- The Strategic Response Matrix assesses and categorizes threats based on their impact probability and time to materialization, aiding in prioritizing and allocating resources effectively.

- The Strategic Response Canvas offers a structured approach to crafting responses to identified threats, enables effective communication with senior leadership and stakeholders and fosters a culture of strategic thinking.

PART II

Do Things at Scale

"Design for spread and scale."

—Denise Gershbein

Leaders periodically need to focus on enhancing their team's capabilities through technology investments. A significant part of this is the ability to communicate and justify technology investment decisions. Clearly articulating the rationale behind these technology investment decisions— such as selecting the right design software, upgrading communication platforms, or adopting data visualization tools–ensures transparency by enabling team members to understand and engage with the decision-making process.

Managing the technology portfolio is a critical aspect of effectively scaling internal capability. The tools covered in this section will equip design leaders with the ability to assess their current technology investments, identifying areas of over- or underinvestment. This assessment allows for the reallocation of resources to optimize the impact of technology on design operations and it ensures that investments meet current needs while remaining scalable for future requirements.

Retaining design talent is a key focus of building team capability. After all, you can't build capability while simultaneously losing talented individuals and their organizational knowledge. Team members who feel more connected to the company's mission and goals are more likely to stay. The more they see the value and impact of their work on the organization, the stronger their connection becomes. We will learn strategies to develop each team member's career path, tailored to their engagement level and competencies. This personalized approach to career development seeks to retain talent by fostering a culture where designers feel valued, motivated, and inspired to contribute.

"Do Things at Scale" is about empowering leaders to strengthen their teams through strategic technology investments and effective portfolio management, while nurturing and retaining design talent by aligning their career growth with the organization's vision and goals.

CHAPTER 5

Enhancing Team Capabilities with Advanced Tools

At this point, we have established a strategic direction, identified potential threats, and put risk mitigation strategies in place. Now, we need to build the knowledge and skills required to achieve our objectives. To enhance our capabilities, we may be considering multiple solutions. In this context, "solution" refers to any technologies, systems, processes, and skills that improve the organizational capability.

The next step is thus about evaluating the solutions. *How do we decide which solution is best? What criteria are we using? Does this effectively build the capability needed to support our chosen approach?* This is where we can use a decision matrix. A decision matrix can be applied to a wide range of scenarios to provide a more structured approach to decision-making.

In this chapter, you will learn

- What is a decision matrix?

- How to systematically evaluate options against weighted criteria

- How to facilitate collaborative decision-making and stakeholder buy-in

© Garkay Wong 2025
G. Wong, *The Art of Design Strategy*, Design Thinking,
https://doi.org/10.1007/979-8-8688-0552-3_5

Streaming Wars: How Disney Tried to Challenge Netflix's Dominance

I first started streaming as a college student in the late 2000s when Netflix was still the new kid on the block, and my classmates and I all shared subscriptions to save on costs. Netflix, if you're reading this, these were entirely legitimate "group study sessions." Over time, more people made the switch from cable TV to streaming. Attracted by the increased convenience and flexibility, no need for a physical box, as well as the absence of TV ads made it a superior experience. With 277 million subscribers as of 2024, Netflix has established itself as a global powerhouse, one of the most valuable media firms, and the undisputed king of streaming.

Other entertainment companies looked at Netflix and thought they could copy its success. Apple and Amazon Prime jumped into the ring, but Disney became Netflix's most formidable competitor. With the launch of Disney+ in 2019, Disney capitalized on its vast library of beloved content from franchises like Marvel, Star Wars, Pixar, and Disney Animation. The service attracted millions of subscribers quickly, thanks to its family-friendly offerings and exclusive new content like *The Mandalorian* from the Star Wars universe. Disney's massive catalog was also bolstered by acquisitions like 20th Century Fox and Hulu, giving it a strong competitive edge.

However, Disney has faced financial pressures, and despite rapid growth in subscribers, it has struggled with profitability in its streaming segment. In recent years, Disney has had to cut back on content spending to manage losses and increase subscription costs, which has slightly dampened its momentum.

A Winning Technology Approach

Netflix has always been known for its technological approach to content, integrating machine learning and data-driven algorithms to recommend content to its viewers, which the other streaming platforms have since copied. By analyzing viewer behavior—such as watch time, interactions, and preferences—Netflix tailors individual recommendations. This personalized experience has been essential in keeping users engaged, ensuring that they can easily discover new content that matches their tastes.

Beyond mastering the art of engagement, Netflix also uses the data it gathers to greenlight projects it knows will be successful. For example, since Netflix knows how many people watch true crime shows, they created a show called *Monster*, focusing on notorious serial killers. These AI tools help inform decisions about new projects and ensure that content investments align with what audiences want. AI also helps with the design of promotional images and trailers, quickly generating variations to see which resonates most with different demographics.

Another Netflix success is the ad-supported tier, adding additional revenue and making it more affordable for users tired of paying for multiple subscription services. In late 2023, Netflix reported that 30% of all new signups were on this ad-supported plan. Disney+ and Amazon Prime have watched closely and decided they would offer their own ad-supported tiers, copying Netflix's model.

While other streaming services have used technology to innovate, Netflix has emerged as the winner of the streaming wars. Despite facing increased competition from services like Disney+, Amazon Prime, and HBO Max, Netflix has maintained its dominant position in terms of subscriber numbers and profitability. Currently, it has more than 277 million subscribers, adding 30 million new subscribers last year, and it continues to lead the streaming industry with its broad content library and international reach.[1]

---

[1] Clark, Travis, "It's been a year since Netflix launched its ad tier. Here's what advertisers can expect next." The Current, 4 Nov. 2023, `www.thecurrent.com/netflix-advertising-streaming-amazon-media`.

A Lesson in Investing in Priorities

One of the key reasons for Netflix's success is it knows what to invest in and how to make tough decisions. In March 2017, Netflix embarked on an ambitious journey to streamline its subtitling and translation efforts through the launch of Hermes, a translation portal. Its aim was to attract top-tier translators globally to meet Netflix's growing localization needs. Hermes allowed translators to test their skills and potentially join Netflix's subtitling workforce, making it a critical piece of Netflix's broader strategy to make its content accessible worldwide. However, the program was short-lived. By March 2018, Netflix announced the platform was shutting down. While Hermes succeeded in onboarding many translators, Netflix realized that managing the recruitment, training, and onboarding of thousands of translators was beyond its core strengths.

As a technology company, Netflix's main competencies lie in content localization workflows, engineering, and platform development. In contrast, recruitment and onboarding are tasks at which its localization vendors excel. Therefore, Netflix decided to pivot, allowing these vendors to handle the recruitment process while Netflix focused on refining its technology and processes. This decision allowed the company to shift resources back to where they could deliver the most value.

However, despite shutting down the program, the project generated several valuable ideas that continue to shape Netflix's localization efforts, including highlighted improvements in scheduling, style guides, and Netflix's cloud-based localization platform. The platform has also become more responsive to feedback from localization professionals, with feature requests like spell check, autocorrect, and translation memory integration making their way into future development plans.

The Design Technology Investment Matrix

Decision matrices are tools that can be applied to a wide range of decision-making scenarios. Companies can use them to make better informed decisions regarding expensive, potentially irreversible investments such as choosing technology infrastructure, determining site selection, or selecting software solutions. In these cases, you want to be sure you've carefully weighed all the options and considered all the important factors before committing to a direction (and a significant investment!).

In the early 2000s, Disney was working on selecting the location for one of its new theme parks. This decision was critical because, once made, it required a significant investment of resources. Naturally, they needed to get it right and carefully evaluate all available options. At the time, they were deciding between locations such as Hong Kong, Shanghai, and several other cities in Asia. To make the best choice, they followed a structured decision-making process—identifying potential locations, setting clear criteria, and weighing each option against those criteria. Similarly, the same structured approach applies to decisions around technology infrastructure today. Table 5-1 provides an example of how a decision matrix could be applied to a major tech infrastructure choice.

Table 5-1. *Cloud provider selection using a decision matrix*

Criteria	Weight	AWS	Azure	Google Cloud
Cost	25%	4	3	5
Service offerings	20%	5	4	3
Scalability	20%	5	4	4
Security	15%	4	5	4
Ease of Use	10%	3	4	5
Support	10%	4	5	3
Total	**100%**	**4.30**	**4.00**	**4.05**

While I can only speculate about the exact internal decision-making process for determining the technology approach for the Disney+ streaming platform, this is how it might have played out using a decision matrix. The Matrix consists of two key components: the Options under consideration and the Criteria for evaluation. By systematically assessing each option against established criteria important to various stakeholders, it ensures all perspectives are considered.

The first key component of a decision matrix is the Options under consideration. In Figure 5-1, we have broadly defined the technology investment options as: buy, configure, outsource, build in-house, or acquire. These were chosen as starting points rather than leaving the options undefined. The rationale is that these five choices encompass the major routes organizations take when adopting new technologies.

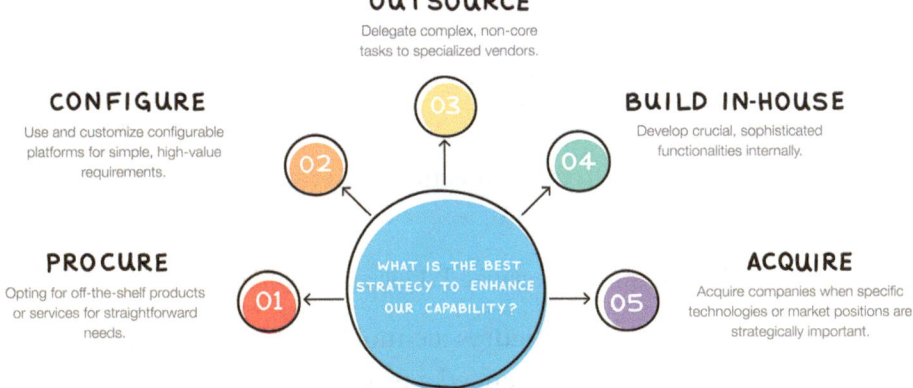

Figure 5-1. *Technology adoption criteria*

The five options under consideration in this case are as follows:

Procure

Procurement involves purchasing ready-made software solutions for immediate use.

- Pros: Quick deployment, lower initial costs, and proven solutions.

- Cons: Limited customization and potential dependency on vendors.

Example: Disney likely uses off-the-shelf software for non-core functions like payment processing in Disney+, ensuring quick deployment and cost-effectiveness.

Configure

Configuration includes modifying existing technologies to meet specific needs.

- Pros: Flexibility in customization, potential cost savings, and adaptability.

- Cons: May require specialized skills and could be time-consuming.

Example: Disney likely configures technologies like the MagicBand system in its theme parks for enhanced guest experiences.

Outsource

Outsourcing involves hiring external companies to handle certain technological functions.

- Pros: Access to specialized expertise and affordable talent scalability, and focus on core business. Outsourcing also reduces operating expenditures (OPEX).

- Cons: Less control over development, potential quality issues, and reliance on third parties.

Example: Disney likely outsources certain IT functions or cloud services for scalable infrastructure.

Build In-House

Building in-house involves developing technology internally from scratch.

- Pros: Total control, customization to specific needs, and integration with existing systems.

- Cons: High up-front costs, resource-intensive (increases OPEX), and longer development time.

Example: Disney developed its streaming service in-house, allowing full control and customization.

Acquire

Acquisition involves purchasing other companies to acquire their technologies.

- Pros: Immediate access to advanced technology, market expansion, and competitive advantage.

- Cons: High cost, integration challenges, and potential culture clashes.

Example: Disney's acquisition of Hulu is an example of acquiring technology to expand its streaming capabilities and market reach.

Navigating Complex Technology Investment Decisions

Maybe you've been here before—design leaders, executives, and key stakeholders are gathered in an open, vibrant office space adorned with colorful Post-it notes and sleek glass partitions. The room is humming with excitement and tension. They are here to discuss the future technology direction of their business. In this critical meeting, the CEO, or perhaps another C-suite executive, presides, listening intently to the varying perspectives.

In this scenario, it falls upon the design leader to present the advantages and disadvantages of various technology investment options, all while considering the multifaceted criteria of the stakeholders. Each decision, whether it involves procurement, configuration, outsourcing, in-house development, or acquisition, brings an array of benefits and hurdles.

At these meetings, it's likely that financial stakeholders will question the design leader's decisions, especially if they lean toward a more costly or innovative approach that doesn't reflect their own priority for cost-efficiency and/or rapid deployment. IT representatives might also raise concerns if the decision appears to conflict with existing systems and infrastructure. The CMO might have strong opinions on overall brand positioning or alignment. The challenge: forging a strategic consensus that caters to diverse priorities.

In a situation like this, you often end up with a clash of personalities, with the loudest person in the room either winning the argument or drowning the others out. But it could be (and often is) that Quiet Sally sitting in the corner of the room has the killer insight or incisive perspective that could have a major strategic impact.

There sits Quiet Sally—holding the figurative map to the company's future—all while the CFO is yelling at everyone about controlling costs. The CTO and CIO meanwhile are bickering about what technology to invest in and who has ownership over which tech stack. The CMO is busy shouting words like "synergy" and gesturing with "jazz hands" while the CEO tries to figure out how to work the intercom so he can tell his secretary to push back his three o'clock.

This is where a decision matrix can help to bring calm to the room by structuring and reframing the conversation to consider everyone's diverse viewpoints. Instead of shouting about which projects are more important, the stakeholder can engage in a structured and open discussion to determine the relative importance of the different criteria by which those projects should be assessed.

The design leader might present insights around a project's impact on the customer experience (CX) and how this might boost growth, bolstered by the Chief Marketing Officer who underscores the project's longer-term market positioning. This might lead the CFO to reevaluate their initial focus on raw cost and balance their perspective with a view on the cost of not investing in the project. By understanding the broader impact and future benefits, the CFO might agree that the lowest cost option might not align with the company's long-term strategic goals.

The group reaches a consensus, rating strategic value and developmental control as their highest priorities at 5/5. Brand positioning, IP security, and cost are deemed moderately important, each scoring 3/5. Other criteria are assessed for their importance, falling between these extremes on the scale. See Table 5-1 and Figure 5-2 for examples.

Once each criterion is assigned a weight, the options are assessed against the specified criteria. The scores are then calculated by multiplying them with their corresponding weights. The recommended option, with the highest total score, aligns most closely with the identified needs and priorities.

This decision matrix brings significant benefits to the technology selection process. Rather than limiting discussion to a trade-off mindset of fast deployment, low cost, or innovative capabilities, it facilitates an integrated approach where it may be possible to fulfill multiple criteria simultaneously. If a trade-off must be made, there is at the very least wide consensus and understanding about why.

Additionally, the decision matrix provides critical documentation of the rationale behind the final decision. If questioned in the future about why a certain selection was made, design leaders can reference the scores and trade-off discussions captured in the matrix. This level of transparency and explainability builds confidence and trust in the decision-making process.

By tallying the scores for each option and seeing clearly how they compare, the decision matrix makes the conversation less about opinions and personalities and more about objective evaluation. This leads to better, more balanced decisions and secures buy-in across the organization. Ultimately, the decision matrix reframes traditional decision paralysis into an opportunity for consensus-building and forward progress.

Solving the Right Problems with Clear Criteria

 Greg Solomon is an actuary, a business advisor, and an author. He has extensive international experience and currently lives in Hong Kong. He believes strong communication is the secret sauce of most success.

It's alarming how often a solution fails, or the wrong solution is implemented, simply because everyone wasn't clear on what problem was being solved. Of course, everyone is convinced they know—and agree—what the problem is but often such conclusions are too superficial to drive the right solution and design.

There is a big difference between "increase sales" and "increase sales in the female mid-income 40-60 ages range." And, of course, "improve the user interface," "speed up the user interface," and "reduce drop-off rates during user on-boarding" each requires different solutions.

When speaking with the client, it's important to remember that what they "want" and what they "need" are often different, and if we can't bridge that gap during our discussions, we are at risk of producing designs which, although they meet the initial spec, they fail to move the client.

Successful design strategy is built on having clarity about the problem.

—Greg Solomon

💡 Tool Tips: Why Decision Matrices Beat "Gut Feel"

Our brains can only comfortably assess a couple criteria at once when making decisions. For instance, when I order dinner on a food delivery app, I go by craving and affordability, selecting whatever I happen to be in the mood for or what is cheapest. But I'm missing important criteria, and I end up overeating fatty foods.

Structured decision matrices counter this human constraint by enforcing evaluation across balanced weighted criteria simultaneously. For my dinner, that could mean parameters like healthiness, taste, budget, and waste generated. Scoring options across 5+ factors results in optimized meals—maybe a homemade veggie quinoa bowl. This trumps decisions skewed by an emotional fixation on taste or cost exclusively, as my brain intuitively does when unsupported by structure.

The matrix integrates a broader range of inputs than what our innate judgment can manage alone, leading to more responsible choices. It enables decision-making that extends beyond impulse or convenience, resulting in well-considered and defensible choices.

When my husband asks me why we are eating veggie quinoa bowls for dinner instead of steak, I can give a well-reasoned argument supported by nutritional benefits and long-term health considerations. It helps us choose something that may seem less emotionally appealing in the moment but will be better for us in the long run, allowing us to move from making good decisions to making the best decisions. Of course, this is just an example of how decision matrices could be applied—I'm not actually using one to decide every meal, nor am I holding my husband hostage with quinoa bowls.

Practical Application: The Technology Adoption Canvas

The Technology Adoption Canvas is a tool designed to guide organizations in evaluating and deciding on technology adoption strategies. It combines analysis with strategy, enabling decision-makers to make informed decisions about technology choices.

Key benefits include

- Facilitates Buy-in and Discussion:

Encourages active participation and open discussion among stakeholders, leading to greater consensus and commitment to the chosen technology strategy.

- Balances Strategic Considerations:

Incorporates a broad spectrum of criteria, ensuring that technology decisions are comprehensive and align with a wide range of immediate and future-focused organizational goals.

- Enhances Transparency and Justification:

Provides a clear and logical framework for decision-making; the Canvas ensures technology choices are transparent and well-justified.

The Technology Adoption Canvas

The Technology Adoption Canvas is a decision-making tool designed for evaluating technology options against criteria weighted and agreed upon by stakeholders, facilitating informed, collaborative decisions on technology adoption.

Technology Adoption Canvas   Instructions: Determine whether you should buy, configure, outsource, build in-house, or acquire technologies to enhance capability.

Criteria	CRITERIA WEIGHT	PROCURE	CONFIGURE	OUTSOURCE	BUILD IN-HOUSE	ACQUIRE
STRATEGIC VALUE	5	2	3	2	5	4
INTELLECTUAL PROPERTY	3	2	3	1	5	4
BRAND POSITIONING	3	2	3	2	5	4
COST	3	4	3	3	2	1
SYSTEM INTEGRATION	5	1	3	2	5	4
DEVELOPMENTAL CONTROL	4	2	4	3	5	3
TOTAL	-	47	73	50	106	79

Figure 5-2. *Technology adoption canvas*

Components of the Technology Adoption Canvas

- Criteria: Factors crucial to the decision

- Weights: Importance level of each criterion

- Options: Technology adoption strategies such as Buy, Build In-House, etc.

- Scoring: Rating each option against criteria

Step 1: Define the Question or Problem Statement:

- What is the overarching question or problem the decision matrix aims to solve? In this example, the overarching question is "What is the best strategy to enhance our capability?"

127

Step 2: Identify Options or Alternatives:

- What are my options? Here we have defined the options as Buy, Configure, Outsource, Build In-House, or Acquire. These five choices encompass the major routes organizations take when adopting new technologies.

Step 3: Establish Criteria:

- What are the factors crucial to the decision? As a group, decide the criteria that are important to the decision. For example, these might be: Development Control, Cost, System Integration, Strategic Value, Brand Alignment, Technical Debt, and IP.

Step 4: Assign Weights:

- What is the importance of each criterion? Each participant assigns a weight to these criteria based on their importance. In this scenario, weights are measured on a scale of 1 to 5, with 5 being most important. Higher weights signify greater importance to the organization's objectives and needs. These weights can also be expressed as percentages (totaling 100%), but this is a matter of analytical preference.

Step 5: Rate Each Option Against Criteria:

- How well does each option meet the established criteria? Evaluate and rate each option against the defined criteria, using a consistent scale. This process involves a detailed assessment to determine the relative importance or priority of each option in relation to the criteria.

Step 6: Calculate Totals:

- How do the options compare when scores are weighted? Multiply the scores for each option by their respective weights, and then add these values to get a total score. Examine the total scores to ascertain which option aligns most effectively with the defined criteria and weights.

Step 7: Make a Decision:

Which option has the highest score? Choose the option with the highest total score, as it best fulfills the identified needs and priorities.

Workshop Introduction: Navigating Technology Adoption with the Decision Matrix

Understanding the Current Situation:

What factors should influence our decision to Buy, Configure, Outsource, Build In-House, or Acquire new technology? How do these decisions align with our strategic objectives and operational capabilities?

The Role of the Canvas

We'll use the Technology Adoption Canvas, a structured tool to help us evaluate and decide on technology adoption strategies. The canvas facilitates a methodical approach to analyze various options like Buy, Configure, Outsource, Build In-House, or Acquire, against crucial decision-making criteria.

Workshop Objectives

- Define Criteria: Identify and agree on the factors critical to the technology adoption decision.

- Assign Weights and Rate Options: Determine the importance of each criterion and rate the technology adoption strategies against them.

- Calculate Totals and Make Decisions: Use the weighted scores to evaluate options and make informed decisions.

Participant Selection

The ideal number of participants for this workshop is between 6 and 8, which enables senior stakeholders to actively participate while still representing diverse viewpoints.

For a workshop evaluating significant technology investments or platform decisions, senior executive involvement is crucial to ensure that the rest of the organization understands that the technology adoption strategy has top-level buy-in. This reduces the likelihood of arguments further down the chain. For smaller technology commitments or contained-scope decisions, the participant level can be scaled down as appropriate. For an executive-level technology strategy alignment workshop, key stakeholders should include those found in Table 5-2.

Table 5-2. *Key stakeholders*

Department	Roles
Senior Management	Chief Executive Officer (CEO) Chief Operating Officer (COO)
Finance and Risk	CFO (Finance and Risk) Head of Risk Management
IT	CTO (IT) CIO
Design	Chief Design Officer (CDO) UX Strategist Lead
Marketing	Chief Marketing Officer (Marketing)
Others (Optional)	Chief Compliance Officer (Governance/Compliance) General Counsel (Legal) Chief Human Resources Officer (HR)

Preparing for the Workshop

- Materials Preparation: Print individual A3-sized copies of the Technology Adoption Canvas for each participant and one large A1-sized copy for group activity. Provide Sharpies and Post-Its.

- Logistics Setup: Arrange a conducive space for group work and discussions.

- Create an agenda (Table 5-3).

Table 5-3. *Agenda*

Rundown			Time
09:30–09:45	Introduction	Overview of technology adoption challenges and the Decision Matrix approach.	15 mins
09:45–9:50	Canvas Tool Briefing	Guide participants on how to use the canvas	5 mins
09:50–10:20	Define Criteria and Weights	Step 1: Define Criteria: As a group, discuss and agree on the key factors crucial to the technology adoption decision.	30 mins
		Step 2: Assign Weights: As a group assign weights to these criteria on a scale of 1 to 5.	
		Step 3: Define Options: As a group consider different technology adoption strategies.	
10:20–10:50	Assign Scores	Step 4: Rating Each Option Against Criteria: Individually rate how each option meets the established criteria using a consistent scale.	30 mins
		Step 5: Take each participant's individual scores and average them out across the group. Put this group average score on the A1 canvas.	

(*continued*)

Table 5-3. (*continued*)

Rundown		Time
10:50–11:20	Identify the Best Options	Step 6: Calculate Totals: Multiply scores by weights for each option, then sum these to get total scores for each strategy.	30 mins
		Step 7: Preliminary Decision: Groups identify the option(s) with the highest total score as the best fit for the organization's needs.	
11:20–11:40	Group Discussion	Teams discuss the proposed strategy based on their canvas.	20 mins
11:40–12:00	Conclusion	Recap key insights and next step actions.	20 mins

After the Workshop

- Documenting Decisions for Future Reference: Create a comprehensive record of the technology adoption choices made during the workshop. This documentation should include the rationale behind each decision, the criteria used, and the weighting and scoring process.

- Email Summary: Distribute a summary of the workshop findings and decisions.

- Implementation Teams: Assign teams to execute the chosen technology adoption strategy.

- Continuous Review: Set up a process for regular review and adjustment of the technology strategy.

The Technology Adoption Workshop enables design leaders and executives to align on technology investment decisions validated through participative analysis. Using a weighted Decision Matrix in the workshop, stakeholders evaluate strategic options against agreed organizational criteria to select the optimal technology adoption approach. Hands-on involvement from the CEO, CTO, and CFO drives future buy-in to resource its execution.

Key Takeaways

- As evidenced by Netflix, for companies to succeed, they must recognize their core strengths and limitations. While innovation and ambitious projects are important, knowing when to pivot or shut down initiatives that don't align with a company's expertise is crucial for long-term success. In Netflix's case, they realized that managing large-scale translator recruitment and onboarding was outside their strengths, so they made the tough decision to end the Hermes program and focus on what they do best.

- Using a decision matrix can simplify complex technology investment decisions. By systematically evaluating options against weighted criteria, these matrices help ensure objective and consensus-driven choices.

- The Technology Adoption Canvas is a tool for evaluating technology options against stakeholder-agreed criteria, facilitating informed, collaborative decisions, and bolster stakeholder buy-in.

CHAPTER 6

Design Investment Prioritization and (Re)-allocation

For over a century, Ford built its reputation and business around gasoline-guzzling vehicles. However, as global environmental regulations tightened and younger consumer preferences shifted toward sustainable options, Ford faced a critical decision: Should it continue relying on its profitable internal combustion engine (ICE) vehicles or pivot to electric?

This shift required reallocating resources, announcing it would phase out several traditional vehicle lines and channel significant investment toward EV development. This included developing the all-electric Ford Mustang Mach-E and F-150 Lightning. Ford committed over $1.9 billion toward electrification efforts, even though it meant scaling back on ICE research and development, a difficult move for a company deeply rooted in traditional car manufacturing.

The decision wasn't easy and isn't without controversy. However, the strategic shift enabled Ford to stay competitive in a rapidly changing automotive industry, positioning it as a major player in the growing EV market.

© Garkay Wong 2025
G. Wong, *The Art of Design Strategy*, Design Thinking,
https://doi.org/10.1007/979-8-8688-0552-3_6

There may be times when exceptional circumstances cause a major shift in priorities and tough decisions are needed. Although this is a situation none of us want to face, it's important to make informed decisions about where we can reallocate resources from projects that no longer serve our goals. While it's often a tough call to make, it's our responsibility to ensure our teams have sufficient support to deliver on the most important strategic initiatives.

In this chapter, you will learn

- What is the Investment Prioritization Model?

- How to adapt digital strategies in response to external factors

- How to reallocate resources from underperforming projects to those with greater strategic value

Optimizing Your Portfolio of Digital Initiatives

Let's imagine a hypothetical scenario for a moment. Put yourself in the shoes of a VP of Digital Design for a large UK grocery retailer. You're in charge of a portfolio with a mix of customer-facing design initiatives made up of apps, websites, and experimental services like grocery delivery. Suddenly, the economic climate in the UK takes an unexpected turn— the aftereffects of Brexit, changing oil prices, global conflicts disrupting supply chains. Given the tight margins that grocery chains already operate on, your design initiatives are under threat. How do you make decisions around which initiatives to prioritize?

Faced with the financial pressures of rising grocery costs and the demands on our capacity to maintain app operations, it is clear that we need to rethink our approach. Because you've done your TRACES homework, you'll have an idea of the relevant threats and new opportunities presented by shifting audience trends. You respond to two customer demands: the need for locally sourced goods and for affordability. Instead of continuing to allocate resources to enhancements that do not differentiate the app from competitors, you propose a feature that promotes locally sourced products on your app—showcasing local farmers, artisans, and producers—and detailing the journey from farm to table to helping consumers gain a deeper appreciation for the food they purchase.

Within a year of this strategic realignment, the app differentiates itself from competitors in the market by meeting a growing demand for sustainability, connecting customers with a variety of local produce and homegrown brands that support the local economy. This reduces the company's reliance on expensive imports, decreases transportation costs, and enhances resilience to supply chain disruptions, which allows the company to pass the savings on to the customer.

The Investment Prioritization Matrix helps organizations assess projects by capacity and strategic fit to ensure they're making the best use of their resources as situations evolve. It forces organizations to think critically about whether the project is truly aligned with the company's long-term strategic goals and whether it has sufficient resources to deliver the benefits. Using the tool, you see that spending and allocation of resources on the underperforming collection service can be reduced, which will ease further losses. Available capacity can be shifted toward building a feature that highlights locally sourced products. This complements the collect-in-store service because it allows customers to conduct their research at home, browse local products, and use the collection service to conveniently pick up their selected items in-store.

Balancing Fit and Capacity

Investment Prioritization empowers design leaders to methodically evaluate and compare design initiatives by focusing on two key aspects: strategic fit and delivery capacity.

There will always be tension around what needs to be done, when it needs to be done, what can feasibly be achieved, and when it can be achieved. When resources are limited, companies must make hard decisions and be selective about which projects to invest in. For instance, a financial services company could invest in expanding to other markets, growing the sales and marketing team, developing a mobile app, updating the website, improving their fraud detection models, or building an innovation lab. Companies with large portfolios of investment decisions can easily have dozens of such projects competing for the same limited pool of resources.

Utilizing Investment Prioritization can help us think beyond quick wins and focus on the projects that offer the best balance between available resources and what is needed for a company's future growth.

The Investment Prioritization Matrix is an approach to decision-making that focuses on whether our design efforts contribute to and are aligned with a company's strategic objectives, rather than how much effort it requires. It helps provide a clear rationale for making resource decisions aligned with strategic growth and ensures high-value design projects get the resources they need to succeed.

For instance, a project might be so important to the company's long-term growth that it justifies expanding capacity—through hiring or reallocation of resources—to see it through. Design leaders can make informed decisions about where they need to scale capacity and make a case for more high-impact projects, rather than dismissing them just because they require a lot of effort and/or money.

When we align to strategic fit, we can be more discerning about where to deploy resources and which projects will drive future growth. We might decide to allocate more resources to those projects that are so important for a company's growth (or survival) that it might justify additional investment or time to build the capacity to meet those challenges head on. Keep in mind that capacity is not static; it can and should be built up and adjusted over time according to the changing needs of the organization. Understanding the strategic fit helps ensure that when we are asked to respond to new challenges or capitalize on opportunities, we can deploy our resources effectively to achieve those outcomes.

Strategic Alignment Guides Precision

Evaluating strategic fit and capacity is not just about recognizing which projects align with our goals, it's also about creating a strong rationale for why these projects are worth pursuing. Design leaders are increasingly being asked to justify the value of their work through precise measurements such as Return on Investment (ROI) and other business-related metrics. However, these numbers do not always fully capture the strategic value of design work. Before we focus on precision, we must ensure we're moving in the right direction. This is why being "strategically right" should precede being "precisely" right. Both are important but direction and alignment must create the foundation for precision to follow.

Precision in numbers doesn't always translate to effective decision-making, especially if the underlying strategy is misaligned. For example, Return on Investment (ROI) calculations, KPIs, and other performance metrics are precise but can be misleading if they don't consider the strategic context. Design projects are multifaceted, and they influence the business in ways that are not always quantifiable or easily measured. The difficulty of tracing business outcomes back to the experiential aspects of design adds to the challenge of properly attributing credit to design initiatives. Executives often hold the belief that "we would have gotten there even without design," and the assumption that a great result was a fait accompli.

For design leaders, the ability to demonstrate strategic alignment is the golden ticket to proving that design interventions are doing the right thing—without having to go down the rabbit hole of precise ROI calculations. This approach speeds up the decision-making process and ensures that senior leaders are briefed on the issues they care about most while keeping the discussion aligned.

However, there will be times when a more exact dollar figure might be needed, especially when engaging with CFOs or other stakeholders who prioritize exact numbers or when a business case is required to get funding for an initiative. This is where being "strategically right" can help bridge the gap. After aligning your efforts, resources, and initiatives to broader organizational goals, you can then estimate costs based on known values. While you can't really say how much a given project costs, if you know the exact amount for one project, you can extrapolate by comparing it to any other project in terms of strategic importance and capacity.

This is beneficial not only in understanding costs but also in highlighting the expected benefits, which are often key for decision-making and funding. Linking costs to strategic value can build a stronger case for investment by clarifying how much each project costs and what to expect in return. This way, while strategic alignment has the main stage, design leaders can cater to stakeholders who need financial details as well.

Aligning Our Decisions with Our Strategic Objectives

Ian Richardson has worked in the field of real asset management and investment planning for over 25 years. He has authored industry frameworks to help sectors formalize their investment decision making approaches. He has a research interest in risk perception and how it drives corporate behavior.

Why is investment decision-making so challenging for so many businesses and why—as decision-making moves away from board level and percolates down through the business—do decisions become misaligned with the strategic objectives the board was aiming to achieve?

Having served as a member of the investment executive in a large utility company, I reviewed countless investment appraisals all seeking the group's approval for implementation. In my early experience, I grew frustrated that it was always very difficult to compare the relative benefits of what were often a diverse suite of investment proposals being tabled for our consideration.

In the utility context, there was a disconnect between delivering a project and understanding the proportion of tariff income that would be secured/generated by that project in the future, meaning that many of the key financial appraisal techniques were difficult to apply with any accuracy and became subjective. Different parts of the business and different individuals therefore presented the perceived benefits of their investment proposals in a variety of ways. More often than not, the more experienced senior and charismatic engineers got the approvals they sought, owing to the way they confidently extolled the merits of their schemes. On the other hand, those less confident in their delivery would often leave disappointed, despite the merit in their proposals.

(continued)

Aligning Our Decisions with Our Strategic Objectives

It wasn't long before the group identified the need to have a more structured way of talking about risk and developed a framework that would provide a quantifiable and consistent means for evaluating the benefits of proposed investment options. We ensured that the content of the framework aligned entirely with the strategic objectives laid down by our board to ensure that those projects that provided the best alignment to delivering those objectives were prioritized in our investment decision-making processes.

The group insisted that this framework was not only used to support decision-making at the strategic level but also applied when it came to evaluating tactical decisions. This kept our tactical decisions better aligned with the strategic objectives and removed a culture of adding additional scope into the project, often driven by the mantra that "seeing as we have mobilized, we may as well do x, y, and z while we are here." Where those scope changes added cost but not value against those criteria that really mattered, they became much easier to identify and manage.

We also recognized that certain aspects of performance in our framework were more valuable than others, not only to the business but its customers and other stakeholders. Building in these relative differences in perceived value from different groups enabled a more nuanced evaluation to be undertaken.

Adopting a formal investment prioritization approach, aligned with managing those risks that could otherwise prevent the business from achieving its strategic objectives, is a cornerstone of effective investment planning. It helps companies deliver the suite of investments that best serves their interest and provides decision-makers within the business the means to justify their decisions in a fair and quantifiable way.

—Ian Richardson

Decoding the Investment Prioritization Model

The Investment Prioritization Model (Figure 6-1) is a simple tool for evaluating design initiatives and investments, based on an assessment of the two factors of Strategic Fit and Capacity. Capacity refers to the available resources of the design team (time, money, people) while Strategic Fit assesses how well a project aligns with the desired service outcomes. Finding the right balance means pursuing important projects within the team's capacity to execute.

Using this matrix, you can evaluate design initiatives and place them within these quadrants, allowing teams to discern how each initiative aligns with strategic objectives and how effectively it is being executed.

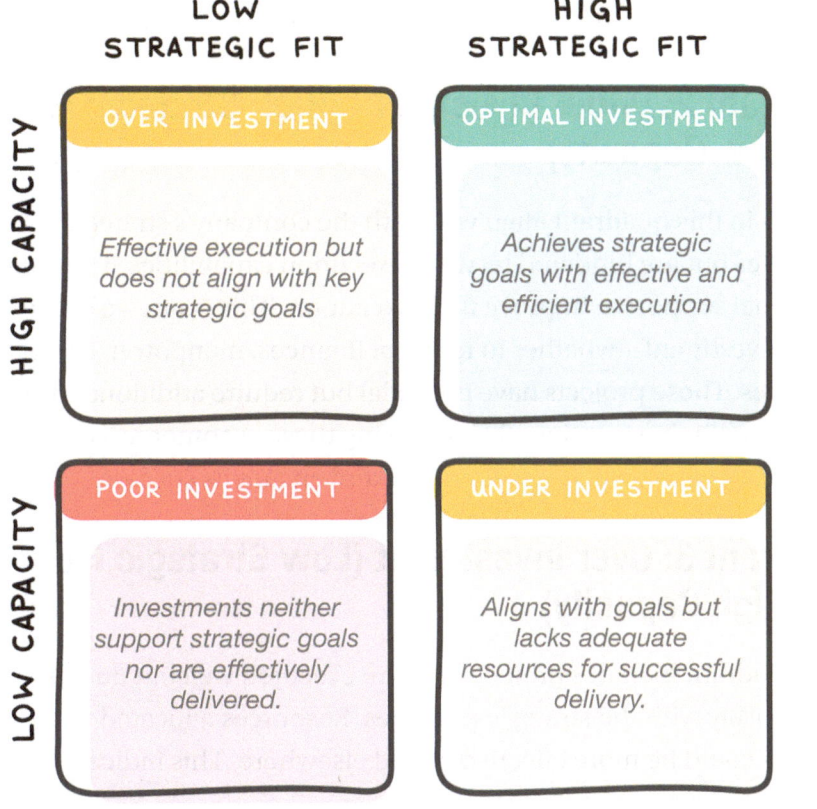

Figure 6-1. *Investment Prioritization Model*

Now we will look at the four quadrants of the Investment Prioritization Model.

Quadrant 1: Poor Investment (Low Strategic Fit and Low Capacity)

This quadrant represents projects that have low alignment with the company's strategic goals and suffer from weak execution capabilities. Investing in these projects can lead to a waste of resources and opportunity. These are essentially poor investments because they neither support the company's long-term vision nor are they likely to be successfully completed. The logical action for these projects is clear: They should be discontinued since they offer little value and drain resources.

Quadrant 2: Under Investment (High Strategic Fit and Low Capacity)

Projects in this quadrant align well with the company's strategic objectives but are hindered by weak execution capabilities. They require additional support to improve their execution. This is often a sign of underinvestment—whether in terms of finances, manpower, or other resources. These projects have potential but require additional support to improve their execution. By identifying these, a company can redirect resources to enhance its development and ensure its success.

Quadrant 3: Over Investment (Low Strategic Fit and High Capacity)

This quadrant includes projects that are executed well but do not align closely with the strategic priorities. Resources allocated to these projects could be more effectively used elsewhere. This indicates an overinvestment in areas that, while they may be successful operationally, do not contribute optimally to the company's strategic objectives. Resources allocated to these projects could be more effectively used elsewhere.

Quadrant 4: Optimal Investment (High Strategic Fit and High Capacity)

Projects in this quadrant are strategically aligned with the company's goals and are delivered effectively. These investments represent the ideal use of resources that contribute to the organization's success. They should be prioritized and maintained.

This matrix helps identify which projects are receiving disproportionate resources, whether overinvested or underinvested. Understanding these dynamics enables design leaders to make informed decisions about reallocating resources without needing to know the precise cost of projects. By doing so, they can optimize the impact of each project, ensuring that investment aligns with strategic value and delivery effectiveness.

The Investment Prioritization Model not only identifies weak spots in investment but also pinpoints opportunities for better resource allocation. Notably, situating projects within this matrix is not a hard-and-fast rule—rerunning the model periodically might result in variation due to changes in sentiment or circumstances. The data nerds like my husband call this "sensitivity"—I call it an opportunity to have a structured conversation around priorities.

Practical Application: The Investment Prioritization Canvas

The Investment Prioritization Canvas is a simple tool for evaluating and optimizing design efforts, ensuring that they contribute maximally to the organization's success by aligning with strategic priorities and effectively utilizing resources.

Key Benefits of the Canvas:

- Guides Decision-Making Toward Strategic Goals:

  The canvas steers decision-making processes toward the organization's strategic goals. This guidance is invaluable for aligning design initiatives with broader business objectives.

- Assesses Design Initiatives for Strategic Fit and Capability Strength:

  The canvas provides a framework to evaluate design initiatives based on their "Capacity" and "Strategic Fit." This assessment ensures investments are operationally sound and strategically aligned.

- Offers Direction for Resource Allocation:

  Instead of focusing on precise ROI figures for each design initiative, the canvas offers a clear direction for resource allocation. This approach is useful for identifying areas where the organization might be over- or underinvesting.

- Emphasizes Strategic Direction Over Tactical Precision:

  The method used in the canvas emphasizes the importance of being "strategically right" rather than "precisely wrong." This focus on strategic alignment over detailed metrics helps avoid decisions that might be well-calculated but strategically misaligned.

The Investment Prioritization Canvas

The Investment Prioritization Canvas (Figure 6-2) is a decision-making tool designed for evaluating various technology options against criteria weighted and agreed upon by stakeholders, facilitating informed, collaborative decisions on technology adoption.

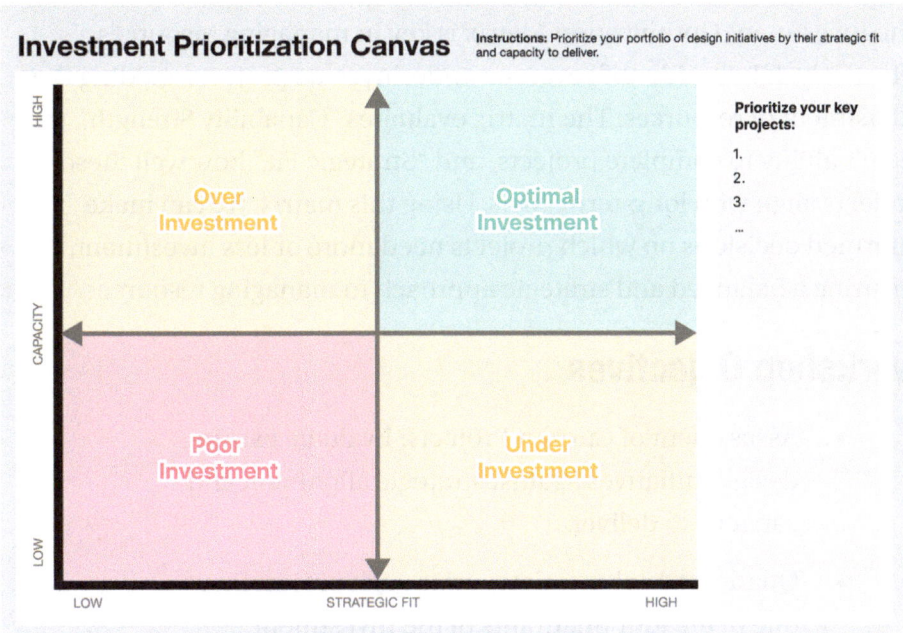

Figure 6-2. *Investment Prioritization Canvas*

Workshop Introduction: Optimizing Design Investments

Understanding the Current Situation

In the face of external forces like market changes or budget cuts, design projects often encounter the challenge of resource reallocation. Similar to the UK grocer example mentioned earlier in the chapter, we might experience a budget reduction, necessitating the reassessment of ongoing projects. This situation demands a focus on aligning design initiatives with the organization's strategic goals while ensuring their feasibility in terms of execution. Essentially, it involves evaluating which projects can still thrive with limited resources and determining which are crucial to the company's objectives.

Role of the Canvas

The Investment Optimization Matrix is key in managing resources effectively. It helps identify over- or underinvested projects, guiding the adjustment of resources. The matrix evaluates "Capability Strength," the team's ability to complete projects, and "Strategic Fit," how well these projects align with long-term goals. Using this matrix, we can make informed decisions on which projects need more or less investment, ensuring a balanced and strategic approach to managing resources.

Workshop Objectives

- Assessment of Current Projects: Evaluate existing design initiatives against strategic alignment and capacity to deliver.

- Quadrant Analysis: Categorize each project into one of the four quadrants of the Investment Optimization Matrix.

- Resource Optimization: Identify overinvested or underinvested projects and strategize on reallocating resources for optimal impact.

Participant Selection

The ideal participant size for the Investment Prioritization Workshop is between 8 and 12. For a comprehensive approach, it's essential to include the CFO for their crucial role in budgeting and financial oversight and senior roles like the COO and CDO for strategic direction and high-level decision-making. Directors or heads of departments such as IT, Marketing, and HR also play a key role, offering strategic insight and detailed operational knowledge. Table 6-1 lists who should be included.

Table 6-1. *Workshop participant list*

Department	Roles
Senior Management	Chief Operating Officer (COO)
Governance/Compliance	Compliance Director
Finance and Risk	Chief Financial Officer (CFO)
Legal	Senior Legal Advisor
Human Resources	Senior HR Business Partner
IT	IT Director/Senior IT Manager
Design	Chief Design Officer (CDO) Design Manager
Marketing	Marketing Director
Others (Optional)	Chief Data Officer Product Development Manager Customer Relations Manager Operations Manager

Preparing for the Workshop

- Materials Preparation: Print a large A1 size Investment Prioritization Canvas, Sharpies, and Post-Its.

- Logistics Setup: Arrange a conducive space for group work and discussions.

- Create an agenda (Table 6-2).

Table 6-2. Workshop agenda

	Rundown		Time
09:30–09:45	Introduction	Overview of the Investment Prioritization Matrix	15 mins
09:45–9:50	Canvas Tool Briefing	Guide participants on how to use the canvas.	5 mins
09:50–10:20	Group Mapping Activity	Participants use the matrix to evaluate and categorize projects into the four quadrants.	30 mins
10:20–11:20	Group Discussion	Discuss the placement of projects, focusing on those that require attention for reallocation or adjustment.	60 mins
11:20–11:50	Strategy Development	Develop action plans for reallocating investments where necessary.	30 mins
11:50–12:00	Conclusion	Summarize key insights, decisions, and next steps.	10 mins

After the Workshop

- Actions Documentation: Compile a detailed report of the matrix outcomes and the strategic plans for each project.

- Follow-Up Meetings: Schedule regular meetings to review the progress of the reallocation strategies and make necessary adjustments.

We can use the output from the Investment Prioritization Workshop to help ensure resources are well-aligned and allocated strategically. By involving of COO and department heads in decision-making, their concerns can be considered. Also, senior leaders can have confidence that efforts and resources devoted to this initiative are aligned toward achieving the organization's goals. The workshop and its output can help simplify the challenge of navigating budget constraints and discussions.

Key Takeaways

- The importance of adapting digital strategies in response to external factors is evident from examples of companies struggling with the volatility of events like Brexit, fluctuating oil prices, and supply chain disruptions.

- Investment Prioritization balances resource allocation between strategic fit and delivery capacity. It ensures support for high-value projects while reallocating resources from or discontinuing low-value projects that do not align well with strategic goals.

- The Investment Prioritization Matrix is a structured tool for assessing a portfolio of digital initiatives. It allows you to select a portfolio of projects that optimizes the overall investment impact.

CHAPTER 7

Building and Retaining Design Talent

When Elon Musk purchased Twitter for $44 billion, he underestimated the value of one of Twitter's greatest assets: the knowledge and expertise of its 7,500 employees. Without this talent, X, as it is now called, is just a shell of a company with office space, some patents, a brand (albeit a damaged brand) that lacks the ability to innovate, iterate, and refine. Musk didn't help matters by making design and functionality changes without consulting anyone. While we don't have definitive numbers now that X is a private company, the company has displayed a clear decline in advertising dollars and users. According to an article in the Washington Post, X's investors have lost billions of dollars, with Fidelity valuing the X stake as 70% below its purchase price.[1]

There are a few key lessons here: First, companies that see employees as mere cogs in a machine risk catastrophic mistakes. When leaders treat employees as replaceable parts rather than valued contributors, they undermine morale, creativity, and loyalty. The result can be talent flight, operational disruptions, and a loss of institutional knowledge. Employees are the core of any organization, and disregarding their contributions or

---

[1] Siddiqui, Faiz, "Musk's Twitter Investors Have Lost Billions in Value," The Washington Post, 1 Sept. 2024, www.washingtonpost.com/technology/2024/09/01/musk-twitter-investors-underwater/.

© Garkay Wong 2025
G. Wong, *The Art of Design Strategy*, Design Thinking,
https://doi.org/10.1007/979-8-8688-0552-3_7

failing to nurture their growth can have far-reaching consequences on company stability and future success.

In this chapter, you will learn

- How the TRACES framework can help inform design teams about the strategic rationale behind certain business decisions

- How organizations can leverage the Career Growth Matrix to boost employee alignment and engagement

Aligning with Your Purpose

Think back to a time when you worked on a project you were passionate about. What made that project special for you? Take a minute and reflect on it. Now, think of a time when your work didn't feel rewarding or impactful. Why was that? Perhaps you experienced feelings of frustration, aimlessness, and a disconnection from the broader goals of the company. These emotions often stem from inadequate communication about how your work fits into the larger strategic picture.

When priorities are misaligned, or their importance isn't clearly communicated, it can lead to a sense of working in a vacuum, where the significance and impact of your efforts is not clear. For instance, when management alters the scope of a design project, designers might complain about management's lack of design understanding. What they might not know is that management might, for instance, have been driven by a concurrent and competing initiative to update legacy IT systems on the back end.

If communication breakdowns are not addressed, it can reduce motivation and satisfaction and lead to poorer outcomes. Recognizing and addressing these alignment issues is important to ensuring that design work is fulfilling for the designer and beneficial for the company.

Understanding and Addressing Design Team Grievances

Misalignment with corporate objectives can bubble up as grievances from designers. These grievances, if left unaddressed, can lead to decreased motivation and engagement. For instance, when designers express concerns that "management doesn't understand design," this could be a result of Technical Debt (T) necessitating design adjustments that seem arbitrary but have a higher strategic priority. Similarly, the pressure of "tight timelines" can stem from Economic Trends (E) and a company's need to adapt quickly to market changes. These are just a couple of examples of how grievances might be tied to TRACES elements.

When everyone in the organization, from the top down, is aligned with the strategic priorities of the company, it can create a more cohesive and effective work environment. Of course, there are instances where these issues stem from poor leadership or executive incompetence, but let's focus on what designers can fix!

To achieve the golden thread of alignment, effective communication is essential. Leaders play a pivotal role in bridging the gap between design work and corporate goals. Strategic objectives must be clearly communicated and demonstrate how design initiatives contribute to these aims. When designers can see how their work fits into the bigger picture, they feel more connected to their projects. This can unlock their full potential and lead to better business outcomes.

Table 7-1. *Addressing designer concerns with TRACES*

Designer concerns	TRACES aspect	How TRACES can provide clarity on strategic priorities
"Why are we even redesigning this feature?"	Regulatory Changes (R)	Some design requests may stem from the need to comply with new regulations. For example, a request to redesign the entire onboarding process might seem arbitrary but could be a necessary adaptation to changing regulatory requirements.
"The goalposts keep moving."	Competition (C)	In a competitive market, businesses must adapt quickly. What seemed like a priority yesterday might change based on competitor moves. Recognizing this dynamic can reduce frustration.
"They want it done yesterday."	Economic Trends (E)	Economic pressures, such as a downturn, can accelerate timelines as businesses rush to adapt. Understanding the big picture can make the reason for these tight deadlines more apparent.
"Why am I always the last to know?"	Audience Shift (A)	Market conditions and shifting user needs can lead to rapid changes in design direction. Understanding the importance of these shifts helps designers recognize why decisions are made, reducing feelings of being out of the loop.

(*continued*)

Table 7-1. (*continued*)

Designer concerns	TRACES aspect	How TRACES can provide clarity on strategic priorities
"Management/IT doesn't understand design"	Technical Debt (T)	Recognizing that some features or redesigns are prioritized to address underlying technical issues can give clarity. More than aesthetics, it's about ensuring the product is technically robust and future-proof.
"Is my job under threat? I can't keep up with best practices."	Substitute Technologies (S)	Embracing new technologies requires continuous learning and adaptation. With the TRACES framework and innovation embedded within the design team, designers are supported in staying updated with emerging technologies. This structure reduces fear and uncertainty about technological changes, fostering confidence and growth.

By contextualizing design concerns within the TRACES framework, designers are better positioned to understand the rationale behind business decisions. With this knowledge, they can more effectively anticipate change.

1. Technical Debt (T):

    Understanding: Recognizing the limitations of current technical architecture.

    Impact: Enables designers to anticipate and adapt to technical constraints, fostering closer collaboration with the development team for feasible and innovative solutions.

2. Regulatory Changes (R):

   Understanding: Being aware of evolving legal standards impacting the product or service. Regulatory changes can impact the onboarding process.

   Impact: Helps designers respond proactively to changes in compliance, avoiding costly redesigns and legal issues, enhancing their role in risk management.

3. Audience Shift (A):

   Understanding: Identifying changes in user behavior and preferences.

   Impact: Equips designers to adapt designs based on changing needs and preferences, emphasizing the importance of feedback and user testing in creating user experiences that resonate.

4. Competition (C):

   Understanding: Recognizing competitors' influence on design decisions.

   Impact: Provides context for prioritizing features, inspiring designers to create differentiated and impactful solutions.

5. Economic Trends (E):

   Understanding: Grasping the impact of economic conditions on the business and users.

   Impact: Prepares designers to adapt to budget and timeline changes, underscoring the importance of economic decision-making.

6. Substitute Technologies (S):

    Understanding: Recognizing the emergence of new
    technologies.

    Impact: Inspires designers to experiment with
    cutting-edge solutions, keeping the design team at
    the forefront of innovation.

From a business standpoint, aligning employees to corporate
objectives ensures that creativity and innovation are properly and
professionally managed. This translates into tangible benefits, such as
higher productivity, reduced waste of resources, and cost efficiency. For
design teams, engagement extends beyond job satisfaction; it reflects their
passion and commitment to their work. Companies that actively showcase
the value of design create a culture where designers feel appreciated.
For instance, when companies like Apple prioritize strong design values,
it not only enhances brand equity but also signifies to employees that
their creative efforts are core to the company's identity and success.
Recognizing this sets the stage for tackling questions of career growth.
While we've discussed managing grievances as an important aspect of
retaining talented individuals, it is as or more important to provide them
with a clear path to achieving their career ambitions.

The Career Growth Matrix

Jensen Huang, the CEO of Nvidia, one of the most profitable companies
in the world, emphasizes a leadership philosophy focused on continuous
improvement rather than firing employees for poor performance. Contrary
to the philosophy of more hardnosed CEOs, Huang prefers to invest in
employees by teaching them how to excel. He believes in fostering growth,
often remarking that people are just a step away from achieving greatness,
and that it's the leader's responsibility to guide them across that threshold.

In a now-famous interview, Huang humorously shared, "I'd rather torture you into greatness," meaning he will go to great lengths for employees to reach their fullest capabilities.

The 9-box talent grid, a framework for assessing and developing talent within organizations (Figure 7-1), is widely used by HR professionals in talent management. However, it is flawed because it depends on highly subjective judgments, often leading to favoritism and bias. There are many versions of this tool, but typically it consists of a 3x3 grid where one axis represents performance and the other represents potential. Each axis typically ranges from low to high, creating nine distinct boxes where employees can be categorized based on their perceived performance and potential.

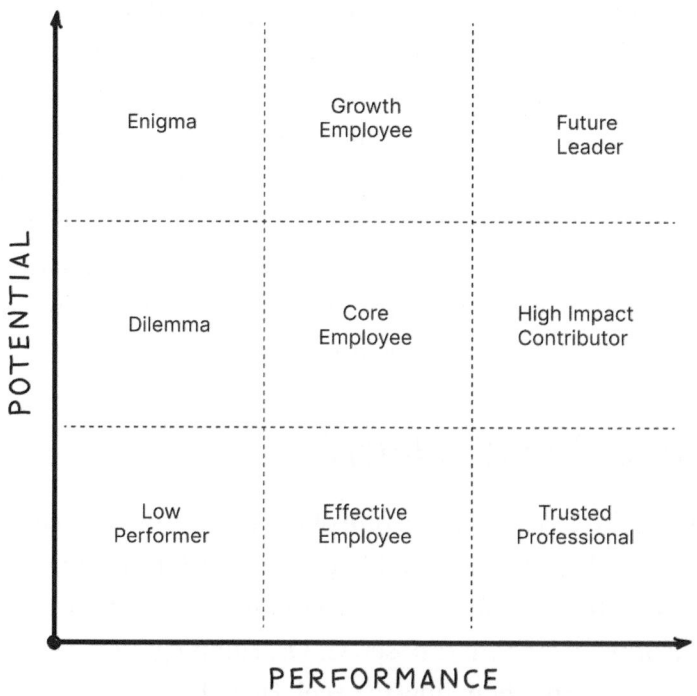

Figure 7-1. *Example of the 9-box talent grid from "The Management Institute"*

Many individuals worry about their job security and performance evaluations like the 9-box talent grid can heighten this anxiety. On the performance axis, employees are evaluated based on their past achievements, contributions, and results. This axis assesses how well employees have met their job responsibilities and achieved objectives. However, past achievements are not always reliable predictors of future success.

The potential axis gauges an employee's future capabilities, readiness, and suitability for more senior or challenging roles within the organization. Yet, this dimension introduces a significant challenge: individual manager bias and the inherent subjectivity in projecting future potential. Managers' assessments of potential can be influenced by personal preferences, prejudices, and limited perspectives, resulting in questionable judgments.

The issue is that we are all human. When, for instance, interpersonal conflicts impact the quality of work output, managers are not always skilled at distinguishing these subjective factors from actual performance factors. In other words, they're biased. This introduces inconsistencies in the evaluation process, as managers may have differing perspectives on what influences performance and what constitutes potential. These may be influenced by a manager's personal preferences or prejudices.

The potential turnover costs associated with these outdated talent management practices cannot be ignored. Huang would probably underscore the need for a more holistic approach to talent management, one prioritizing alignment with organizational goals and capability development.

The Trust Factor: Overcoming the Fear of Feedback

 Tracy Myers has been based in Hong Kong since 2013 and has held numerous global leadership roles, overseeing teams in Asia, North America, and the Gulf Region to achieve enterprise goals and talent agendas. She supported the implementation of Gap Inc.'s performance management program's transformation in Asia, transitioning to a new model, processes, and outcomes.

Say the word feedback and it's scientifically proven the threat system of the brain is activated. Why is it so hard to tell someone how they are performing, what they've done well, and what they can do to improve? Most often it comes down to our fear of how we will respond to their response to our feedback—will they be upset? Think less of us? Retaliate? Think about someone you have a great relationship with. You likely trust each other. Now imagine how you need to give them feedback about something you want them to change. It's likely you wouldn't think twice about telling them because you perceive them as a low threat level. Why? You probably have great trust built between you; now, you may deliver that feedback in a bar, as a joke, or while casually making tacos, but the point is you did not have the same level of anxiety as you might with another less-trusted individual.

When we consider the hierarchical and transactional nature of living and working across Asia, we know implementing a behavior and process change for better performance management can be challenging. Why? There's (perceived) comfort (for some) in a highly directive, top-down approach to work. Authority is not questioned, and learning happens in a one-way vacuum. But to change a company's culture requires truly transformative work, and the change management factor can take years, not to mention turnover in talent, cost of training, tools, mental energy, etcetera. So why forge ahead? Because visionary leaders understand the long-term benefits for the company and their employees and have the best interest for both. Not to mention, every generation of employees will require updated ways of working, no matter what part of the globe you're on.

(continued)

The Trust Factor: Overcoming the Fear of Feedback

In the example of updating the performance management program, the shift in behavior and process changes required leaders to stop and think about

1. How often they are engaging in true feedback and

2. What is the quality of the conversation they are having—are they doing all the talking? Are they being specific? Are they acknowledging what they can do better too?

Likewise, the shift required employees to advocate for themselves and critically think about what support they needed from their leader. This was not easy, nor welcomed (Change is hard! I cannot tell my boss what I really think!). However, the employees who began to participate fully in this transformation soon realized they deserved to be heard, that they needed to voice their feedback to get what they wanted, and that the process showed them what kind of manager they really worked for (Do I stay or do I go?). Likewise, those managers who aligned to the new feedback exchange quickly saw an increase in overall team productivity and business performance, better collaboration, better stakeholder feedback and performance, and overall team effectiveness. By no means was it easy, but it was necessary.

—Tracy Myers

Moving away from the performance-by-potential paradigm can alleviate the pressure and anxiety long associated with traditional talent management practices. Performance is backward looking. Capability is future focused. By prioritizing alignment and capability over performance and potential, organizations can support employees in building sustainable and fulfilling careers. This approach emphasizes continuous learning and development, enabling individuals to evolve and adapt to changing business needs. When organizations commit to capability building, employees feel valued and invested in their own professional growth.

The Career Growth Matrix is a framework that assists in identifying where designers stand in terms of their alignment with corporate objectives and their capability in their roles. Assessing employees based on how well their skillset aligns with the organization's goals, values, and strategic priorities ensures they are well positioned to contribute to business objectives. This fosters a sense of purpose and engagement among employees, leading to greater organizational cohesion and effectiveness.

Evaluating employees based on their capability focuses on the development of essential skills and competencies and helps position individuals for long-term success (Figure 7-2). Unlike performance-based assessments, which can be subjective and biased, capability assessments offer a more objective measure of an individual's potential for growth and contribution to the organization.

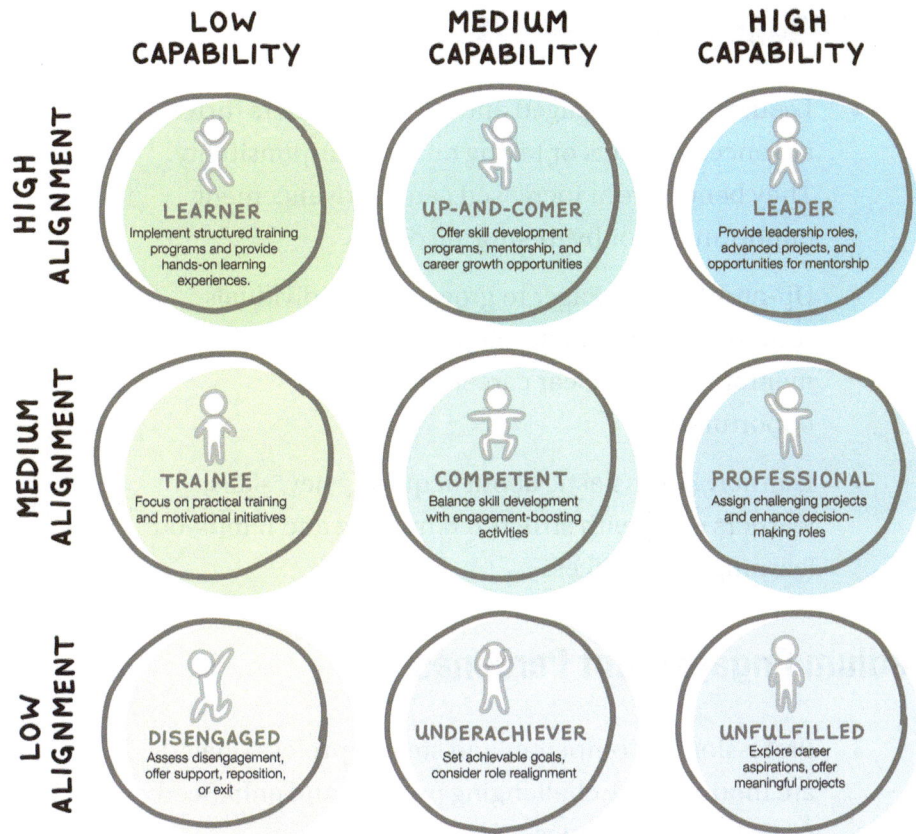

Figure 7-2. *Career Growth Matrix*

The Career Growth Matrix categorizes team members into nine personas, each with unique needs and engagement levels. Understanding these personas helps in tailoring actions and development plans to individual team members more effectively.

High Engagement Personas

- Leader: Highly engaged and capable, leaders thrive on advanced projects or taking on more responsibility. They benefit from increased career advancement opportunities or by mentoring others.

- Up-and-Comer: Eager to grow, these individuals respond well to skill development programs, mentorship, and clear career progression opportunities.

- Learner: Enthusiastic about acquiring new skills, learners excel with structured training and hands-on learning experiences.

Medium Engagement Personas

- Professional: Competent and steady, professionals are motivated by challenging projects and enhanced decision-making roles.

- Competent: Reliable and skilled, they require a balance of skill development and activities that boost engagement.

- Trainee: Newer to the field, trainees benefit from practical training and initiatives that build motivation and engagement.

Low Engagement Personas

- Unfulfilled: These individuals need exploration of career aspirations and assignment to meaningful projects that reignite their passion.

- Underachiever: They may require goal realignment and a reassessment of their current role to better match their skills and interests.

- Disengaged: Addressing the root causes of their disengagement is crucial. This might involve support, a change in role, or even considering an exit if alignment is unlikely to be achieved.

Scenario 1—Enhancing Engagement with Company Strategy

Emily, a talented mid-level designer is known for her exceptional design skills. However, her engagement with the broader company strategy and objectives is limited. While her technical capability is high, she needs development in areas that will help her grow into an effective design leader, such as a strategic thinking mindset and an ability to connect tasks with business outcomes.

Referencing the Career Growth Matrix, the focus for Emily is to enhance her involvement in activities that go beyond her immediate design tasks. This could involve integrating her into strategic planning sessions or involving her in cross-functional teams where she can observe and participate in broader business discussions. Mentorship programs and employee resource groups with a mix of senior leaders and junior employees can also be beneficial. Programs like this can provide Emily with a broader perspective and help her to develop essential soft skills like communication, leadership, and strategic planning to prepare her for more advanced roles.

Scenario 2—Bridging the Capability Gap

Just as we've focused on Emily's growth toward leadership, there are other facets of team development, such as enhancing technical skills. Consider Jack, a new designer brimming with passion for the company's vision but facing a capability gap in technical skills necessary for more complex design tasks. His enthusiasm is valuable, yet his limited experience means he isn't reaching his full potential.

In Jack's case, the Career Growth Matrix can help to pinpoint specific technical areas needing improvement. A targeted training program tailored to his needs, perhaps coupled with a mentorship arrangement, could bolster his technical abilities. Clearly demonstrating the company's investment in his growth helps Jack see a tangible path forward in his career with the organization and map out how he can progress from where he is now to where he aspires to be.

By utilizing this matrix to plot the positions of the entire team, design leaders can gain valuable insights into the overall state of their team's capabilities and overall levels of engagement. This serves as the foundation for crafting talent engagement strategies that address the distinct needs and potential of each team member, as well as the collective needs of the team. A baseline understanding of the current state of the team and its potential can aid development efforts aimed at building diverse capabilities and competencies necessary for the organization to advance its objectives.

Using the Career Growth Matrix sends a powerful signal to employees that the organization is invested in their growth. This shift in approach fosters a more positive environment where employees and employers are aligned in pursuit of larger organizational goals. Traditional models can inadvertently create environments where the narrow focus on performance and potential fosters behaviors characterized by competitiveness and self-interest. Even those who are reluctant to engage in this competitive environment often feel compelled to do so to "succeed," perpetuating a culture where much of the work becomes performative rather than impactful.

In contrast, the Career Growth Matrix moves from judging talent to growing talent. It encourages a holistic view of talent management. By prioritizing alignment with organizational objectives and continuous capability development, the matrix promotes a culture of collaboration, innovation, and mutual support.

Key Takeaways

- Misalignment between design teams and corporate objectives often manifests as grievances among designers, such as perceived lack of understanding from management, confusion about constantly changing priorities, frustration with tight timelines, etc.

- The TRACES framework can address these concerns by providing structured context for explaining the strategic rationale behind certain business decisions.

- Aligning design teams with corporate objectives fosters a greater sense of purpose, engagement, and strategic contribution. Designers can understand how their work impacts broader goals.

- Strategies for boosting alignment and engagement include providing leadership roles, skill development programs, meaningful projects, career growth opportunities, etc., aligned to the team member's position on the matrix.

PART III

Do Things Collaboratively

"Design is a team sport."

—Tim Brown

This part guides leaders in evaluating how design is currently integrated into their organization including how it is perceived and utilized. We will also explore strategies to expand design's impact through strong collaboration across teams. The focus is on deploying the right team types to various scenarios, aligning team compositions and skills with specific organizational challenges and opportunities. This approach enhances the effectiveness and strategic influence of design teams, embedding design more deeply into the organization's operational culture.

Additionally, we discuss how to equip design professionals with the vocabulary and skill necessary to communicate the value of design to senior leadership. This includes methods for demonstrating how initiatives in design practice contribute to business outcomes and for advocating for necessary support and resources. These communication strategies will help elevate the stature of design practice within the organization and ensure its value is acknowledged at executive and management levels.

CHAPTER 8

Adaptive Team Structures for Design Innovation and Creativity

Aligning personal goals with company objectives creates a strong base of skilled individuals. But once these talented individuals are in place, how can we scale their efforts to drive meaningful change?

In this chapter, you will learn the following:

- What are Outcome-based Teams?

- Where in the organization should I deploy design teams for the most impact?

How Adaptive Teams Drive Outcomes

We now turn our attention to how outcome-based teams, made up of talented individuals, can be coordinated to achieve the greatest strategic impact. And what better way to illustrate the impact of team coordination than sport?

© Garkay Wong 2025
G. Wong, *The Art of Design Strategy*, Design Thinking,
https://doi.org/10.1007/979-8-8688-0552-3_8

My husband is an avid fan of Arsenal, a soccer team in the English Premier League. While he was watching a YouTube compilation of "gnarly" sports injuries, he told me about Arsenal striker Eduardo da Silva's horrific leg injury during a high-stakes match in 2008, and, of course, I immediately saw how the story was not just about an unlucky footballer, it was a story about design strategy. Da Silva recalled it as "My worst injury. But I don't want to remember the sadness, just the support that everyone always gave me."[1] His road to recovery and the specialized medical teams that got him back on the field are a powerful reminder of how diverse teams aligned to the same goals can impact physical recovery and leave a lasting emotional impact on the individual involved.

February 23, 2008: Arsenal vs. Birmingham City. Arsenal was poised to win their first league title since 2004. Just minutes into the game, in front of a packed crowd at St. Andrew's Stadium, a Birmingham defender made a reckless tackle, snapping Da Silva's left tibia and dislocating his left ankle. Stunned silence washed over the stadium as Da Silva fell to the ground. The injury was so horrific and graphic that the broadcaster refused to show replays of the incident.

The team's medical staff swarmed onto the field and rushed Da Silva to the hospital where he underwent immediate surgery.[2] A multidisciplinary team of orthopedic surgeons, physicians, and technicians combined their collective expertise to perform the complex surgeries needed to treat his immediate injury. Following the surgery, a team of physical therapists,

---

[1] Silva, Eduardo A. Da (@EduardoDaSilva), "It was exactly seven years ago. My worst injury. But I don't want to remember the sadness, just the support that everyone always gave me. Of course, @Arsenal fans were really special that time. Thanks a lot for everything," X, Feb 23, 2015.

[2] "Eduardo's was a limb-threatening injury"—former Arsenal physio Gary Lewin" Goal, www.goal.com/en-cm/news/eduardo-limb-threatening-injury%2D%2D-former-arsenal-physio-gary-lewin/clf0rx74faz216hto3hh5e7b1.

nutritionists, and rehab specialists created a conditioning regimen designed to return Da Silva to fitness within nine months.[3]

As his needs changed throughout the recovery process, the team responded by providing different types of support as needed. As the months went on and his recovery progressed, attention shifted beyond recovery to include the prevention of future injury, using new biomechanics research and strength training protocols to create a long-term blueprint for protecting his fitness and career. Eduardo's journey highlights the outsized impact of dynamic teams, with each recovery phase enabled by specialized experts aligned around specific outcomes for the patient.

What struck me about this story is how a diverse group of medical and rehab professionals—on the field, in the hospital, and during Da Silva's recovery process—applied their varied skills and approaches to health to aid in Da Silva's recovery. This required each specialist to trust one another to do their respective jobs well. This is what peak teamwork should look like across any organization.

UX designers, writers, researchers, service designers, product owners, content strategists and developers are also capable of collaborating to achieve great things, but it requires trust and focused outcomes. Just like the diverse expertise that aided Da Silva's return to professional football, in business and design, having the right combination of skills and perspectives is crucial for navigating complex challenges and achieving strategic objectives. However, this level of strategic harmony is often missing for design leaders, especially in design-immature environments.

To achieve the greatest impact, it's essential to deploy the right mix of talent to the right problem. Adaptive team structures, as opposed to rigid traditional models, allow for the assembly and disassembly of multidisciplinary talents around specific design efforts. Customer

---

[3] "Fears for Eduardo as Arsenal Predict Nine Months Out," The Guardian, 26 Feb. 2008, www.theguardian.com/football/2008/feb/26/newsstory.arsenal.

expectations are always changing, and what delights them today may be commonplace and ho-hum tomorrow. This is why we need to approach customer needs with flexibility and responsiveness. Just as different specialist teams of medical and rehabilitation professionals adapted to different phases of Eduardo's recovery, design leaders who can coordinate the right mix of talent to address evolving design requirements will better achieve the intended business outcomes.

Business as Unusual: Tapping into Design's Hidden Potential

I have a diverse group of friends spanning different industries and sectors—from finance to architecture to decision science and everything in between. This feeds my natural curiosity about how different fields operate and the tools they use. During a conversation with an actuary friend, he alluded to his leaving corporate insurance because of the long list of failed transformation initiatives he'd witnessed. In reference to his experience, he made a compelling point that stuck with me: "Companies are good at adoption, but not adaptation."

Adoption is easy—implement a new standard or buy a new tool—but the real challenge is whether people will change their behaviors around it. For instance, will they use the new tool correctly or actually fill out all the new data fields in the worklog? This is where many companies falter. They think "We've implemented a new tool and now we can sit back and reap the benefits; problem solved." However, to get the benefits, companies need to change the way people work and interact, and this requires new team structures and mindsets.

Adaptation is an area where the design function can be a secret weapon, a hidden and often overlooked asset within the organization. Other business functions excel at "business as usual." However, when a new tool or standard is introduced, you are introducing change into the equation. Design is, by definition, the discipline most concerned with change, whether driving it or responding to it. Designers excel at rethinking and reshaping how things work. They ask questions and test assumptions to better understand the underlying mechanics of how something works, and then use the insights uncovered to identify opportunities for improvement.

Outcome-Based Teams are a structured way for organizations to better mobilize the skills embedded within the design team to overcome the challenges associated with organizational change. They allow senior executives and design leaders to come together to have a shared conversation around aligning design talent with specific business outcomes.

Introduction to Outcome-Based Teams

Recall the story of Eduardo da Silva's injury. At each step of his recovery, the teams and talented individuals involved were aligned to specific outcomes for the patient. This serves as a great example of Outcome-Based Teams. These teams are formed to address specific challenges or objectives, ensuring that the right people have the needed resources to achieve their aims. By adopting a more fluid team structure, teams are better able to adapt to changing circumstances and respond effectively to new challenges, adjusting their strategies, as necessary.

Whether you are designing or delivering solutions, it's important to have a structured approach that aligns the right type of team to the desired customer outcomes (Figure 8-1). The model consists of four team types—Rapid Response, Precision, Agile, and Strategic. Some of these teams focus on tactical, immediate solutions, while others are more strategic. For example, Rapid Response Teams might be ideal for urgent, short-term projects, responding to unexpected crises or emergencies. Precision Teams can help bring diverse talents across the organization to tackle problems holistically, facilitating ideation sessions and rapid prototyping that leverage the expertise of everyone involved. Agile Teams help drive medium-term strategic initiatives, and Strategic Teams focus on shaping the future with long-term strategic projects. This focused structuring of teams ensures that design capabilities are deployed intelligently and are organized to best solve the challenge at hand.

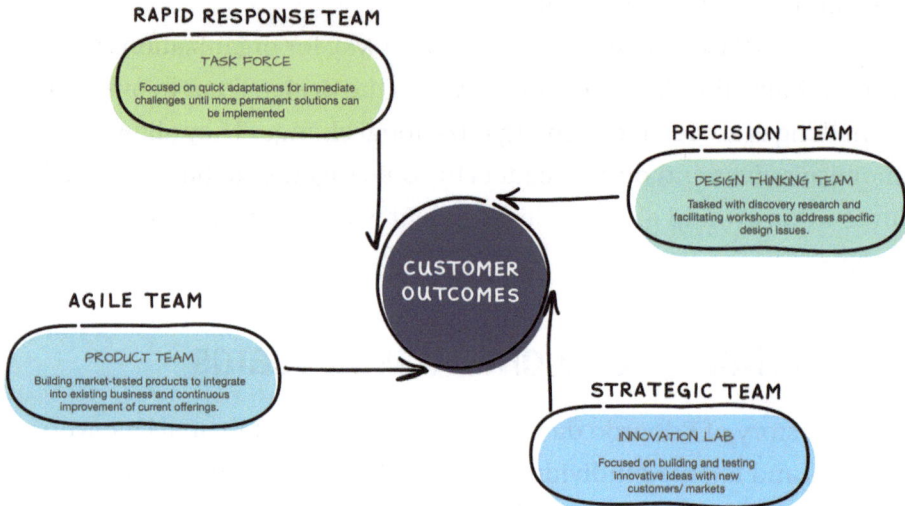

Figure 8-1. Outcome-based teams

The "Outcome-Based Teams" model serves as a guide for selecting the appropriate design team configuration based on an organization's specific needs. This helps identify which type of team is best suited for a given situation, ensuring that the strengths of each team are leveraged for optimal results.

Rapid Response Teams:

> Typically Short-Term, Duration: Days to a Few Weeks

> Capable of quick adaptation, suitable for immediate and prompt responses to emerging threats.

Example Scenario: A task force rapidly implementing social distancing measures in supermarkets during the COVID-19 crisis.

Precision Teams:

Typically Project-Based, Duration: Weeks to Several Months

Tasked with quickly addressing specific design or organizational issues that impact user experience or employee experiences. These solutions are usually co-created to ensure stakeholder buy-in or ensure feedback from customers and employees are considered.

Example Scenario: Design Thinking Facilitation Team for redesigning the employee onboarding experience to improve HR Processes.

Agile Strategic Teams:

Flexible and strategic, able to proactively address medium-term opportunities with a balanced approach.

Example Scenario: Product Teams focusing on developing new software products or features with a medium-term launch goal.

Long-term Planning Teams:

Focused on strategic foresight and long-term planning, perfect for high-impact, long-term opportunities.

Example Scenario: Innovation Labs that concentrate on long-term, strategic projects, such as developing new technologies or exploring disruptive business models.

This categorization of teams enables organizations to properly orient their design resources, ensuring the right blend of capabilities is applied to achieve the desired outcomes.

Expanding Design's Role Beyond Traditional Boundaries

When Apple introduced the iPod in 2001, they didn't introduce a product as much as they introduced an experience. With commercials featuring the music of popular groups like U2 and Gorillaz combined with dancers in silhouette wearing earbuds, this was design strategy at its finest. Soon, the iPod was ubiquitous, and the portable CD Walkman had disappeared.

To be effective, design leaders must identify opportunities for impact beyond the conventional boundaries of the design function. This involves mapping the organization's broader goals and pinpointing where design expertise can play a transformative role. Leaders should look for opportunities to demonstrate impact in parts of the business not traditionally associated with design. Functions like HR, compliance, and customer service can benefit from design thinking, which can offer fresh perspectives.

Once potential areas of impact are identified, the next step is aligning design resources to these opportunities. This requires a careful assessment of the skill mix within the design team and determining what mix can best address the identified opportunities. It might involve forming new cross-functional teams or reorienting existing ones to align with these strategic objectives.

Crucial to this process is fostering collaboration between the design team and other business units. Design leaders should initiate dialogues with other departments to understand their challenges and objectives. Through this collaboration, design teams can integrate their work with broader business strategies.

Finally, for long-term success, embedding the outcome-based approach into the organizational culture is essential. This involves advocating for the value of design thinking across all levels of the organization and showcasing the tangible benefits achieved through this approach. It's about elevating design from a service function to a strategic partner in the organization's growth and innovation journey.

Key Takeaways

- Shifting design priorities emphasize the importance of aligning design teams with customer outcomes, such as enhancing customer experience and driving innovation.

- Outcome-Based Teams help to determine the best mix of talent needed to address specific design challenges, ranging from immediate requirements to longer-term planning.

CHAPTER 9

Advocating for Design Across the Organization

IBM has a long history of emphasizing the importance of design, following the principle that "good design is good business." It's an ethos that dates to Thomas Watson Jr. when he launched the company's first corporate design program. Over the years, IBM invested heavily in design, hiring designers in droves. In 2016, the company trained over 100,000 employees in "design thinking," ensuring the user experience is prioritized in every product decision. IBM's Enterprise Design Thinking program was a transformational approach to apply design thinking to meet its changing priorities, helping reduce development time by 75% and get products to market twice as fast. Despite IBM's recent layoffs, struggles, and realignment, the company is still an advocate for design thinking in serving its customers and increasing its efficiency.

IBM's success highlights that embedding design across an organization requires more than just a top-down directive; it must be integrated into all facets of a company's culture. Different companies will have different levels of design understanding, which means the approach we take to showing design's contribution and value will need to be tailored to those unique circumstances. For companies just getting started, visibility matters; stakeholders first need to see how design works before they buy in to the idea. But visibility alone is not enough. Showing design's value goes beyond just generating and showing off ideas. You have to deliver viable solutions that demonstrably help an organization achieve its ambitions. The value of design only becomes evident when stakeholders recognize its positive impact on their initiatives.

In this chapter, you will learn how to

- Apply the Design Impact Model

- Evaluate the level integration of Design practice within an organization

- Advance the organization to higher levels of awareness and impact

- Cultivate a Design-Driven Culture

What drives a design-driven culture? I recall a conversation with a head of platforms after a particularly successful workshop. We were discussing how some industries embrace design, while others resist. He said, "Design will always be seen as an afterthought until the pain is felt." He pointed to banks and their reckoning moment in the 2008 global financial crisis. That's what pushed them into digital transformation. "Without that kind of pressure," he said, "other industries don't feel the need. They won't embrace design until it hurts."

Companies shouldn't wait until that reckoning moment to adopt a design mindset. Design advocacy can start small—for instance by slowly exposing colleagues to human-centered design techniques in everyday tasks. As mindsets shift to align customer experience to corporate strategy, appreciation for design thinking grows. This emphasis on customer-centricity is integral to decision-making and process development across the company.

However, adopting a customer-first mindset can be challenging. It requires people to move away from process-oriented way of doing things to a more iterative, insights-driven way of working. Departments that are not used to this approach may resist new ways of working that seem unfamiliar or unnecessary. The resistance often involves more than just perceived costs in time or money. Many individuals may resist this shift due to the effort required to change their established routines and processes. Sometimes personal feelings or emotional discomfort are involved. As design leaders, we need to be sensitive to this as we embed design within our organizations.

An organization just initiating design thinking is very different from one where it is deeply ingrained. Companies new to design might be skeptical of the value it brings, which means it's important to set clear expectations up front about what outcomes can realistically be achieved. For example, a company in the early stages of design adoption may limit its design initiatives to sporadic pilot projects. Demonstrating promising outcomes on those smaller projects is crucial for driving wider adoption in the future.

Understanding where your company stands will guide future efforts. The design impact model in Figure 9-1 outlines characteristic behaviors and actionable next steps for each stage.

Features Advantages Benefits

Greg Solomon is an actuary, a business advisor, and an author. He has extensive international experience and currently lives in Hong Kong. He believes strong communication is the secret sauce of most success.

(*continued*)

Features Advantages Benefits

When selling a product, service, or design, we can communicate its upsides on three levels.

First is "Features"—the details of what the product is, what the service includes, what the solution looks like. Second is "Advantages"—the positive implications of our product or service. Perhaps it's cheaper, lighter, faster, more reliable. But we shouldn't stop here. Third is "Benefits"—how the buyer will be better off as a result of those Advantages, which in turn stem from specific features. The Benefit of the solution drives the sale, the acceptance, the take-up. And this is just as true for design as it is for a product you can hold in your hands.

Remember that different people focus on different levels, so not only should we understand our proposed design at all three levels, we should also be clear on who is most focused on which aspect. Indeed, usually the more senior the people we deal with, the more they care about Benefits over Advantages, and Advantages over Features. Mastering this layered approach to communication is key to successful design strategy.

—Greg Solomon

The Design Impact Model

The Design Impact Model is a tool for helping design leaders understand and plan how to scale their design practice within an organization. Using this matrix, design leaders can assess the current state of design practice within their organization, identify which box they fall into, and plan the steps necessary to advance toward higher levels of awareness and impact.

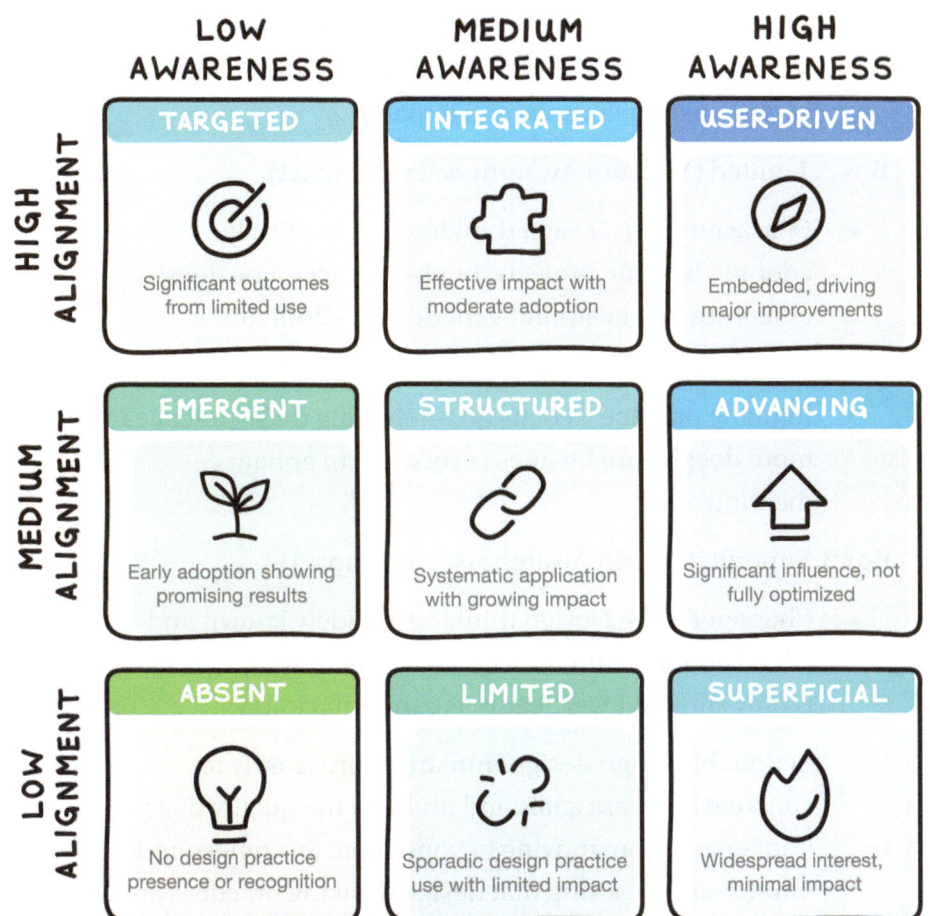

Figure 9-1. *Design impact model*

The Design Impact Model consists of 9 quadrants:

Box 1: Absent (Low Awareness, Low Impact)

- Characteristics: Design thinking and methodologies are either completely absent or unrecognized within the organization. There's little to no emphasis on user-centered design processes.

- Actionable: Initiate awareness programs to introduce the value of design thinking. Implement pilot projects to demonstrate its potential impact.

Box 2: Limited (Medium Awareness, Low Impact)

- Characteristics: Design thinking is sporadically adopted in some projects, but its impact on business outcomes and customer experience is limited.

- Actionable: Standardize and systematize design thinking practices. Focus on integrating these practices more deeply into business processes to enhance their impact.

Box 3: Superficial (High Awareness, Low Impact)

- Characteristics: Design thinking is widely known and talked about within the organization but its application is only surface-level, leading to minimal impact.

- Actionable: Align design thinking more closely to concrete business goals and improve the quality of its implementation, moving beyond mere awareness and interest and ensuring that design thinking practices are effectively applied to solve real business challenges and deliver tangible results.

Box 4: Emergent (Low Adoption, Medium Impact)

- Characteristics: Initial efforts in adopting design thinking show promising results in specific areas or projects.

- Actionable: Capitalize on positive outcomes to advocate for broader adoption of design thinking. Promote the successes achieved through design thinking to increase organizational awareness.

Box 5: Structured (Medium Adoption, Medium Impact)

- Characteristics: Design thinking is systematically applied in various parts of the organization and is starting to show a more noticeable impact on customer experience and business strategies.

- Actionable: Refine and optimize existing design thinking processes. Ensure consistency and high quality in its application across departments.

Box 6: Advancing (High Adoption, Medium Impact)

- Characteristics: Design thinking is a key component of organizational processes and influences business strategies and customer experiences. Its presence is significant, yet there's room for maximizing its effectiveness and improving how that effectiveness is communicated.

- Actionable: Focus on enhancing the depth and breadth of design thinking application. Innovate and adapt design thinking methods to strengthen its strategic role and customer-centric impacts further.

Box 7: Targeted (Low Adoption, High Impact)

- Characteristics: While design thinking is not widely adopted, its targeted application in specific projects or areas has led to considerable and noteworthy positive impacts.

- Actionable: Leverage these high-impact instances as models to promote wider adoption of design thinking. Expand the scope of design thinking practices to elevate their organizational influence and effectiveness.

Box 8: Integrated (Medium Adoption, High Impact)

- Characteristics: Design thinking is not only adopted to a fair degree but also has a substantial impact on business outcomes and customer satisfaction.

- Actionable: Strengthen the integration of design thinking in business strategy. Continue to build its capacity to drive innovation and user-centric solutions.

Box 9: Design-Driven (High Awareness, High Impact)

- Characteristics: Design thinking is deeply ingrained in the organization's culture and processes, driving significant business and customer experience improvements.

- Actionable: Continue to lead with design thinking at a strategic level. Use this quadrant as a benchmark for advancing design thinking in other areas of the organization.

Proposing new structures optimized for flexibility and experimentation can resonate strongly with executives struggling to respond proactively to emerging challenges. Design departments have the unique opportunity to lead the charge. By positioning design as the driving force behind these changes, we elevate the role of design within the organization and empower it to shape the future direction of the business.

Key Takeaways

- Cultivating lasting customer loyalty requires delivering differentiated customer-centric experiences. This involves embracing design thinking widely across the organization.

- The Design Impact Model outlines nine stages of design practice awareness and impact. It assists in evaluating an organization's current design state and determining next steps to advance organizational design maturity.

- Early in the design journey, the focus is on raising awareness and demonstrating value through pilot projects. With broader adoption, the focus moves to better aligning with business goals and improving implementation. The hallmark of a design-mature organization is that business strategy is design-driven.

CHAPTER 10

Influencing Senior Leadership and Decision-Makers

What do decision-makers care about? Senior executives face the daunting task of catering to the needs of two main stakeholder groups—customers and investors. Customers contribute to the company's revenue through their purchases, and investors provide the necessary financial backing for growth. These two groups can have very different (and at times conflicting) priorities, and it's up to the decision-makers to find the right balance. At this stage, we have a good understanding of how our design initiatives align with strategic priorities. We also understand where they provide value, and what mitigation plans have been put in place to manage risk. We can confidently communicate this information to senior leaders to ensure they have the insights they need to balance priorities and meet the expectations of customers and investors.

In this chapter, you will learn

- Lessons from a publicly traded company on the misalignment between investor interests with customer needs

© Garkay Wong 2025
G. Wong, *The Art of Design Strategy*, Design Thinking,
https://doi.org/10.1007/979-8-8688-0552-3_10

- Why traditional metrics like ROI fall short

- How to reframe design value into what decision-makers care about

Balancing Investor Priorities and Customer Needs

A company's success hinges on a clear strategy that embodies its core values. These form the foundation of the brand promise, which plays a crucial role in customer engagement and investor confidence. When customers believe in and connect with the brand promise, it fosters loyalty and engagement. But what if that brand trust is broken?

This scenario played out with Unity, a renowned game engine popular among a broad range of developers, including the indie game community. Their brand promise was so strong that gamers equated games that used the Unity engine, such as Disco Elysium or Among Us, with innovative gameplay that they felt was lacking in mainstream AAA releases. However, Unity revised its monetization strategy due to sustained investor pressure to increase profits. Most of the indie development community was sympathetic to Unity's circumstances and were happy to pay a slightly higher fee. However, Unity failed to consult its customer base and its fee revisions were extremely aggressive, threatening to put indie developers under severe financial strain. This was seen by the community as a betrayal of Unity's longstanding mission of democratizing game development.

As a result, the company faced severe criticism and saw a substantial portion of its customer base move away, culminating in a 15% drop in its stock price[1] in one month and a 25% drop if looking across two months. This situation highlights the perilous consequences of losing sight of customer needs in the pursuit of financial objectives and underscores the importance of maintaining a balance between customer satisfaction and investor expectations in business strategy.

For over a decade, Unity was the go-to engine for indie game developers. Unity positioned itself as affordable and accessible while empowering smaller studios' creativity. This set them apart from its competitor, Unreal Engine, which generally catered to higher budget AAA games. The two engines had neatly carved out their respective niches ... or so it seemed.

This all changed in 2023 when Unity announced a drastic change in its monetization strategy. Unity executives announced plans to raise prices and embed invasive tracking in their game engine.[2] The new pricing model charged royalties based on game installations, ostensibly to align with developers' success. However, this was a poorly thought out approach and raised concerns from developers. Many of these concerns were centered on the tracking system that would be embedded into the engine for the monetization model to work. From a data privacy perspective, developers were concerned about Unity collecting data on end users without their consent, whether this would be GDPR compliant, and therefore whether the developers would be liable for privacy breaches. From a practical perspective, developers had many concerns regarding what would constitute a game installation. Would they have to pay royalties on game reinstallations? Or perhaps even games that were illegally pirated and installed?

---

[1] Lewis, Sophie, "Here's Why Unity Stock Dropped 15% Last Month," The Motley Fool, 3 Oct. 2023, https://www.fool.com/investing/2023/10/03/heres-why-unity-stock-dropped-15-last-month/.

[2] Ivan, Tom, "Unity Is Adding a Royalty Fee Based on the Number of Times a Game Is Installed," Video Games Chronicle, 12 Sep. 2023, https://www.videogameschronicle.com/news/unity-is-adding-a-royalty-fee-based-on-the-number-of-times-a-game-is-installed/.

The developer community raised these concerns in the initial days of the announcement, but Unity had built enough goodwill that the community gave them the initial benefit of the doubt. However, as Unity struggled to answer basic questions about the tracking and charging mechanism, it became obvious that they hadn't put much (or any) thought into the practical implications of their approach. As the backlash mounted, Unity walked back some of its changes—but the damage was done. Wholesale migration began toward Unreal Engine, which was free of such predatory practices. In this scenario, Unreal found an unexpected competitive advantage. By having a simple-to-understand fee model and steering clear of invasive data collection, Unreal earned a reputation for treating developers fairly. Consequently, as trust in Unity eroded, Unreal attracted its indie user base, capitalizing on Unity's error.

This situation was entirely avoidable. Unity's team consisted of experienced developers who very likely understood the long-term repercussions of undermining customer trust and raised these concerns internally. However, these concerns were overshadowed by a myopic focus on immediate financial returns. Unity failed to consider the critical relationship it had with its user base. The shift to a per-install fee model, while financially logical on paper, did not align with the needs and expectations of many developers who relied on Unity. There was a clear disconnect between the business decision and the community's values. If Unity had engaged with its community, they would have found out that developers were happy to accept a moderate price increase to help sustain Unity.

Instead, Unity's decision-makers, focusing on investor interests, leaned almost exclusively on traditional financial metrics like ROI. This neglected insights from team members closer to the customer base. Designers whose job it is to understand the user perspective, might have foreseen the negative reaction from the indie developer community and been able to design a solution that more effectively balanced the needs of investors and users.

Bridging the Disconnect between Design and Business

The Unity case study highlights a common disconnect: financially driven executive decision makers often have competing priorities with customer-facing teams like designers who are attuned to user needs. This is exacerbated by limitations of traditional metrics like ROI in capturing the holistic, long-term value of design. In the context of businesses' growing focus on innovation and differentiation, the significance of design is increasingly recognized, albeit in the abstract. However, design professionals across industries highlight the limitations of traditional financial metrics like ROI in fully capturing design's tangible impact.

The challenge lies in quantifying design's value purely in financial terms, which often doesn't align with the complexities of design practice. This is particularly evident where the role of design is still being integrated and understood. Traditional financial metrics struggle to encompass the nuanced, long-term benefits of design. A key limitation of these metrics is their failure to reflect the qualitative, lasting effects of effective design. In scenarios where the importance of design is still emerging, metrics like ROI often underestimate its true value.

Design influences business performance indirectly, evolves over time, and interacts with multiple business factors, making it difficult to measure through standard financial methods. Notably, the absence of good design can be difficult to measure. Not all instances of poor design thinking result in catastrophe and mayhem. More often, it results in opportunity costs and reduced success. Recognizing these issues, there's an established consensus on the inadequacy of traditional financial justifications for design investments in today's business environment. The following discussion focuses on specific metrics like ROI and explores their limitations in capturing the real impact of design.

Bringing All Voices to the Table

Daniel Lee is a "Jack of All Trades," but his expertise lies in understanding human behavior through user research. He has been a User eXperience Researcher (UXR) for over 8 years and worked for various companies spanning from travel to healthcare. He loves tackling complex spaces and helping teams create better user experiences through user research. When he's not conducting research, you can find him spending time with his wife and four fur babies.

Imagine a crucial strategy meeting but with key players missing. Often, designers and researchers, who hold valuable insights into user needs and market trends, are excluded from these discussions.

This lack of clear communication from leadership leads to a ripple effect:

- Unclear Business Needs: Without a direct line to leadership's vision, managers struggle to translate goals into actionable plans for their teams.

- Misdirected Teams: Confused about priorities, individual contributors (ICs) end up frustrated and spinning their wheels on projects that might not align with the bigger picture.

- Blame Game Blues: When things go sideways, the finger-pointing starts: Designers and researchers feel their input wasn't considered; Managers feel unsupported; ICs feel lost.

The solution? Clearer communication. Leadership needs to bridge the gap by actively including designers and researchers and by equipping managers with a comprehensive understanding of business needs. This can lead to a more focused, collaborative, and ultimately successful organization.

—Daniel Lee

Why We Use ROI in Business Decision-Making

In a 2014 shareholder meeting, a conservative financial group asked Apple's CEO Tim Cook to disclose the cost of Apple's energy sustainability programs in hopes of persuading Cook to focus on more profitable ventures rather than investing in sustainability programs. Cook's response? "When we work on making our devices accessible by the blind," he said, sharply. "I don't consider the bloody ROI."

Widely regarded as a key indicator of financial efficiency in business, ROI encounters a fundamental disconnect when applied to design. Although it is an established tool for guiding profitability decisions across various business contexts, ROI's focus on short-term financial performance carries inherent limitations, especially in design spheres that require a more holistic assessment.

ROI is often used for budget distribution across departments, based on expected returns. By prioritizing activities with high ROI, the theory is that financial discipline is maintained, and resource utilization is optimized - for instance in evaluating marketing campaigns and sales training effectiveness through cost vs. revenue analysis.

The Limitations of ROI in Demonstrating Design Value

A critical issue arises when evaluating investments solely based on ROI. These calculations often emphasize financial return projections, overlooking how an initiative aligns with a company's long-term strategic goals, core values, and brand. For instance, an initiative showing potential for good ROI might still diverge from foundational company objectives. ROI's focus often overlooks the strategic essence of design-driven projects, failing to capture how an investment aligns with the company's broader vision.

While ROI is effective in quantifying near-term financial returns, that focus on near-term gains reveals key limitations in the context of design's qualitative and customer-centric impacts. Aspects such as enhanced user experience, brand loyalty, and potential for innovation carry significant yet hard-to-quantify value not captured in traditional ROI calculations. For example, a well-designed user interface can significantly enhance customer satisfaction and retention but may not translate immediately into financial gains easily measurable by ROI. Retention and satisfaction are fuzzier and less likely to have buy-in from the finance team compared to something that requires fewer or no hoops to quantify, such as increased sales.

The use of ROI as the sole metric for funding also places designers in a challenging position, especially when they lack the tools to connect their activities to measurable outcomes. This situation makes discussions about ROI not only challenging but sometimes impossible. Designers are often tasked with demonstrating the financial viability of creative projects, which can be challenging and counterproductive when the true value lies in intangible aspects like brand perception or user experience.

Traditional ROI evaluations often fail to account for the expenses incurred from halting initiatives that stray from strategic objectives. The initial funds put into these misaligned ventures turn into sunk costs, which are essentially forfeited if the projects are terminated. However, ROI primarily gauges financial gains and doesn't factor in strategic congruence or advancement toward planned results. As a result, initiatives might seem profitable according to ROI but may not contribute meaningful value.

Instead, a measurement on the impact of outcomes on sustainable, long-term profitability can provide better strategic guidance and much needed context to an ROI evaluation. The effectiveness of delivering service outcomes plays a crucial role in sustaining profitability over longer time horizons. Failing to account for outcomes can have significant consequences. When projects are abandoned, it results in wasted resources and missed opportunities, affecting the organization's long-term success. Additionally, since ROI focuses solely on one aspect of output, it offers a limited and at times misleading view of the long-term, qualitative impacts on customer experience, innovation, and other crucial areas.

Rather than relying on detailed ROI calculations, advocacy in design should focus on how initiatives align with overarching business goals and, more importantly, how they deliver meaningful service outcomes to the customer. It is essential for designers to articulate the value of their work in terms that resonate with broader business objectives, emphasizing the customer benefits and long-term brand value rather than focusing on immediate financial returns. Adopting more holistic frameworks is necessary to accurately represent the extensive, enterprise-wide contributions of design.

Beyond ROIs: Design's Outcome-Centric Approach

In contrast to ROI's focus on financial output, design functions prioritize delivering more customer-centric service outcomes. While ROI is primarily concerned with quantifiable financial outcomes, design compels us to ask a fundamentally different, yet essential question: What outcomes did our service deliver to our customers? This question encapsulates the heart of design's purpose—it's not just about the financial return but about crafting experiences that resonate. Given design's unique focus, it is crucial to consider, using the framework and tools we've introduced, what metrics can adequately evaluate the holistic value of design. These metrics should capture more than just financial returns; they should reflect the essence of the customer-centric outcomes that design endeavors to achieve.

Furthermore, to effectively garner executive support and buy-in, it's essential to frame design discussions within the context of these core business concerns. Demonstrating how design directly contributes to and enhances shareholder value, drives growth, optimizes costs, and gives a competitive edge can transform how executives perceive and value design. Designers, therefore, need to develop an appreciation for the pressures and priorities that shape executive decision-making. Translating the language of design into the language of business helps connect design strategies to the company's tactical and strategic objectives. This can build a strong case for the importance of design and positions it as a critical driver of business success.

Speaking the Same Language

While design has come a long way over the years, there is still much work to be done to get executives to understand what design can achieve for a business. This book has hopefully given designers and non-designers a reframing of what design can offer. It's my hope that equipped with the tools and language needed to translate design concepts into business outcomes, we as designers can better meet these challenges head-on.

Improving communication between designers and senior executives requires a cultural shift within organizations. Leadership must acknowledge that design thinking contributes significantly to problem-solving and innovation. When executives understand that design is intertwined with other business functions, they are more likely to support and invest in design initiatives.

Building on the methods, tools, and frameworks introduced in previous chapters, this section emphasizes aligning the entire organization around common objectives such as customer satisfaction and market growth. Creating a cohesive measurement framework accessible to all departments ensures that every segment of the organization contributes to and benefits from these unified goals.

This approach is particularly effective when communicating with executives focused on key business metrics like shareholder return, growth drivers, and cost control. It positions the design frameworks and tools outlined in this book as integral elements within the established business context, thereby facilitating a more effective and collaborative dialogue.

- Shareholder Returns

  This term can be reframed as long-term value creation through design. These tools emphasize creating long-term shareholder value through innovative and user-centric design strategies.

  - Design Maturity Model

    Assessing design maturity enables organizations to strategically target long-term success and shareholder value.

  - Design Impact Matrix

    Assesses the influence of design integration on company growth and market expansion.

- Growth Drivers

  This term can be viewed through the lens of market expansion and diversification through design-led innovation. These tools focus on leveraging design for market growth, expansion, and diversification.

  - TRACES Growth Matrix

    Identifies growth opportunities driven by design-led innovation.

  - Strategy Alignment Canvas

    Ensures effective contribution of design projects to growth plans by aligning them with strategic priorities.

- Cost Controls Tools

  This focuses on optimizing resources and enhancing operational efficiency through design.

  - Investment Prioritization Matrix

    Prioritizes design investments for strategic alignment and impact.

- Competitive Positioning

  These tool said in understanding and responding to market competition and positioning the company advantageously.

  - TRACES Threat Identification Canvas

    Identifies competitive threats and market risks.

  - Adaptive Risk Response (ARR) Matrix

    Prioritizes challenges by impact and likelihood across varied time periods.

  - TRACES Strategic Response Canvas

    Strategizes responses to competitive challenges.

  - Technology Adoption Canvas

    Evaluates the most suitable technological solutions based on various criteria.

- Organizational Dynamics Tools

  This toolset is for understanding and improving team dynamics and organizational structure.

- Career Growth Matrix

  Tool for guiding skill growth and career advancement opportunities.

- Outcome-Based Teams

  Composition of teams assembled to achieve defined goals or outcomes.

- Design Impact Model

  Evaluates the integration of design thinking in organizational culture and identifies opportunities to collaborate cross-functionally.

Key Takeaways

- The common tension between investor and customer needs underscores the necessity of balancing customer and investor interests to maintain a sustainable and resilient business model.

- While ROI resonates with finance functions, it fails to properly evaluate design's contributions to areas like competitive differentiation, customer loyalty, and brand perception, which are critical for lifetime value of a customer and the long-term viability of a business.

- Reframing design language in business terms helps to bridge the communication gap between design and executive functions. This can help designers be better advocates for difficult-to-measure but high-impact design initiatives.

PART IV

Do Things Differently

"Innovation is the ability to see change as an opportunity–not a threat."

—Steve Jobs

Design leaders must build resilient and adaptive mindsets to thrive amidst change and uncertainty. In the long term, designers need to persuade businesses to be both sustainable and profitable if they are to ensure a lasting and positive legacy. This is using design as a "Force for Good."

Design as a "Force for Good" represents the next frontier and requires a reimagining of design's role. Working outside conventional boundaries, designers are empowered to create improved products and services that serve the organization and the community at large.

"Doing Things Differently" is a call to action for businesses to innovate responsibly, urging leaders at all levels of public and private sectors to leverage design as a strategic partner in transitioning toward a more sustainable, equitable future—leading the way to a better tomorrow.

Do Things Differently

CHAPTER 11

Design-Led Transformation for Sustainable Futures

A bold vision, when combined with empirical data, can drive effective decision-making and strategic alignment. Every action, decision, and strategy should be precisely connected with the organization's core purpose. This chapter encourages you to embrace the role of an innovator and perform the hard work necessary to enable your organization to move beyond merely following trends and instead reach for a higher standard as a market leader.

In this chapter, you will learn

- How integrating design principles can transform businesses and drive innovation

- The 7Cs framework which outlines essential conditions for organizations to achieve disruptive innovation

- Design's role in sustainable transformation and leading organizational change

© Garkay Wong 2025
G. Wong, *The Art of Design Strategy*, Design Thinking,
https://doi.org/10.1007/979-8-8688-0552-3_11

Visionaries Driving Transformational Innovation

Henry Ford, remembered for the Model T, was driven by a vision far greater than just creating a car. He once provocatively stated, "If I had asked people what they wanted, they would have said faster horses." This insight reveals Ford's intention to fundamentally change the way people traveled. His introduction of the Model T and the assembly line wasn't just about inventing a new vehicle; it was about revolutionizing the concept of personal mobility and making it accessible to the masses.

Similarly, Steve Jobs' leadership of Apple represents a visionary approach, but with a focus on putting a computer in the hands of everyday people. His approach was not just to create products but to change how people interact with technology. Apple's innovations under his leadership, particularly in personal computers, smartphones, and tablets, were instrumental in redefining how technology can help everyday people do everyday things.

Jobs' vision with Apple shares a fundamental principle with Ford's transformative approach: revolution rather than evolution. While Ford reimagined how products were manufactured, ultimately democratizing the availability of motor vehicles for the masses, Jobs reshaped the relationship between people and computing technology. Neither leader simply improved what was there; they redefined the boundaries of possibility. Their stories remind us of the enduring power of visionary, design-led thinking and show how ambitious goals coupled with adaptive teams can lead to profound changes, often in unexpected ways.

Today's innovation is tomorrow's status quo, which means constant evolution is required to stay ahead of the competition. When you're creating something new, there aren't established rules or a playbook to follow. No one ever "best practiced" their way to innovation because, by definition, there is no best practice if you're first. In the sections that follow, we explore how businesses can draw inspiration from these pioneers, aim for bold ambitious goals and align their organizations around that vision. There are two contrasting but complementary approaches that can shape decision-making and drive results: the normative and empirical approaches (Figure 11-1).

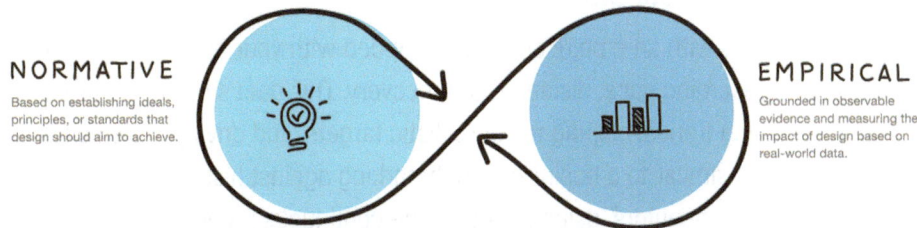

NORMATIVE

Based on establishing ideals, principles, or standards that design should aim to achieve.

EMPIRICAL

Grounded in observable evidence and measuring the impact of design based on real-world data.

Figure 11-1. *The interplay between the Normative and Empirical approaches*

Normative Approach: Normative decisions are often based on ideal scenarios or theoretical best outcomes. This can lead to visionary and innovative choices that aim to push boundaries or set new standards. Normative decision-making is suited for situations with a high uncertainty or complexity in which innovative solutions are needed.

Empirical Approach: Empirical decisions are grounded in data, past experiences, and measurable and observable facts. This leads to more predictable and reliable choices. This approach often leads to incremental changes and continuous improvement, building on what has been proven to work. Empirical decisions might be more easily accepted by stakeholders favoring stability and predictability, while normative decisions might resonate with those seeking transformative change.

💡 Marathon Training: Empirical vs. Normative Approach

Imagine you are setting a formidable goal for yourself: running a marathon. With the challenge set, you decide to combine two distinct training approaches—the empirical and the normative—to ensure you are primed for the race.

Empirical Approach: Data-Driven Training

Your journey begins with an empirical focus. Equipped with your fitness tracker, you log every run—recording pace, distance, and recovery. This data shapes your training decisions, revealing trends, helping to set realistic targets, and driving incremental improvements. It's similar to a business benchmarking against historical performance and competitors, using KPIs to guide continuous progress.

The Normative Approach: Aligning with Theoretical Best

In contrast, your normative approach focuses on achieving the theoretical best outcome within your own limitations and constraints. You consider the fastest marathon time achievable given your age, a 6-month training window, and factors like training hours, nutrition, and rest. This strategy aligns your efforts with an aspirational target. In business terms, it's like aiming to reach optimal potential by aligning strategies with transformative goals, often redefining what's possible through innovation and bold thinking.

Race Day: Culmination of a Dual Strategy

On race day, the combination of empirical precision and normative ambition pays off. Your data-driven training ensures your physical readiness, while your ambitious goal-setting fuels your mental toughness. As you cross the finish line, you realize you've not only completed the marathon but have also exceeded your own expectations.

Often, the highest quality decisions come from balancing both approaches—leveraging data and evidence to guide action while pursuing aspirational goals and innovation. Successful organizations achieve this by addressing both empirical and normative challenges. The empirical approach ensures efficient, effective daily operations, while the normative approach drives transformative growth and defines the organization's values and long-term trajectory.

The 7Cs: Prerequisites for Visionary Innovation

Disruptive innovation is not just about having a single groundbreaking idea but about creating an ecosystem that consistently supports the ideation, development, and implementation of innovative solutions. What were the specific conditions that enabled Ford and Jobs to change their respective industries so fundamentally?

The 7Cs (Figure 11-2) offer a strategic lens through which companies can evaluate and enhance their innovation potential. Addressing each of these areas can significantly increase a company's chances of successfully disrupting markets and establishing leadership in new domains.

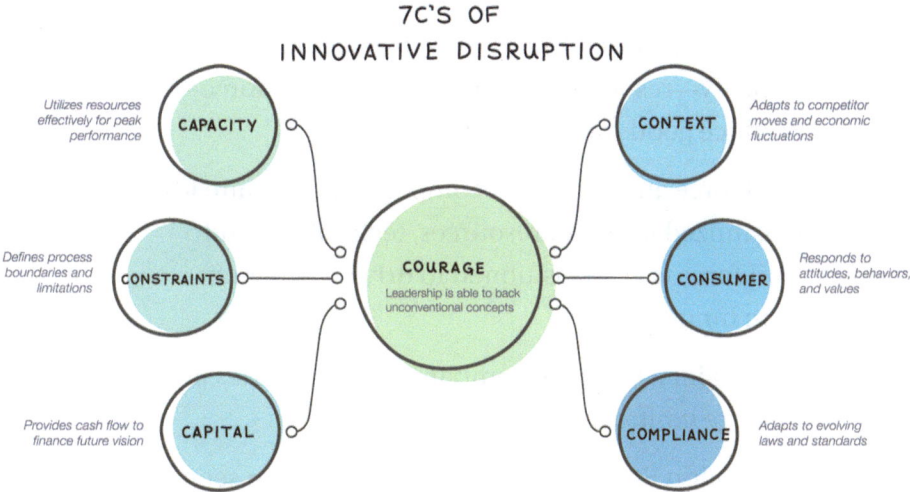

Figure 11-2. *7Cs of innovative disruption. Adapted from Shutterstock*

Each of the 7Cs—Courage, Capacity, Constraints, Capital, Context, Consumer, and Compliance—represents a component in the complex machinery of disruptive innovation. The 7Cs collectively define the prerequisites for a company to transition from a traditional player to a disruptive force in its industry.

1. Courage: Does the leadership demonstrate a readiness to embrace risk and commit to projects that might disrupt existing markets and technologies over the long term?

   Leadership and Risk Management: Innovation requires visionary leaders willing to take calculated risks. Embracing projects that could disrupt existing markets demands a willingness to challenge the status quo, make tough decisions, and stand by them in the face of uncertainty or setbacks.

2. Capacity: Is the company effectively utilizing its capacity—resources, technology, and workforce—to produce goods or services?

   Workforce and Skillset: A company that has already maximized its use of resources, technology, and workforce is well positioned to drive and benefit from innovation.

3. Constraints: Does the company set boundaries and manage limitations?

   Innovation Ecosystem: Constraints are often seen as limitations, but can be an important ingredient in defining the solution space. When companies face restrictions, limitations can actually drive creative thinking which leads to breakthrough solutions.

4. Capital: Does the company have the financial resources available to invest in technology, talent, and other assets?

    Financial Investment: Capital affects the range of options a company has for pursuing its innovation goals. Financial resources are crucial for supporting the research and development of new technologies or solutions. Access to capital allows a company to invest in long-term projects with the potential for high rewards, supporting experimentation and the scaling of successful innovations.

5. Consumer: Does the company have a deep understanding of its consumers, enabling it to anticipate and meet evolving needs and desires?

    Product-Market Fit: Understanding and anticipating consumer needs are critical for disruptive innovation. This requires a deep engagement with current and potential consumers, leveraging data analytics, and empathetic design to uncover not just expressed needs (e.g., "I want a faster car") but also revealed needs (e.g., "I want to get from Point A to Point B faster") that can lead to the development of breakthrough products or services.

6. Context: Can the company address a clear gap or unmet need in the market?

    Market Opportunities: Whether something is considered innovative or not depends largely on the context. Timing, cultural factors, and economic conditions and other factors need to be favorable to allow businesses to enter that specific segment.

7. Compliance: Can the company proficiently navigate through regulatory environments, ensuring its innovative practices align with legal and compliance requirements?

    Regulatory Navigation: The ability to navigate complex regulatory environments is increasingly important in highly regulated industries like healthcare, finance, and energy. Compliance requirements might provide opportunities to innovate when they require companies to develop new processes, technologies, or products.

    The 7Cs represent the foundational elements that enable a company to innovate in a way that disrupts and transforms industries. They are essential for any organization looking to follow in the footsteps of historic disruptors and make a significant, lasting impact in their field.

The Art of Precision Over Power

Achieving maximum impact through focused effort is an ongoing process of alignment, execution, and adjustment. It demands clarity of purpose, strategic thinking, and the flexibility to adapt as circumstances change. My husband, who you already know as an Arsenal fan, was also something of an athlete in his college days. But, no, he didn't sprint across the pitch hunting the perfect curler. He donned a fencing mask, drew a foil, and did his best to outscore his opponents. My husband's anecdotes from his fencing days in college underscore the principle of precision over power (Figure 11-3). He shared that many novice fencers rely on broad, sweeping arm gestures from the foible (the tip or weak part of the blade), mistakenly believing force alone will hit the target. Experienced fencers use their forte (the base or strong part of the blade) and a small wrist motion to push an opposing blade away, while simultaneously keeping the point aimed at and threatening the target at all times.

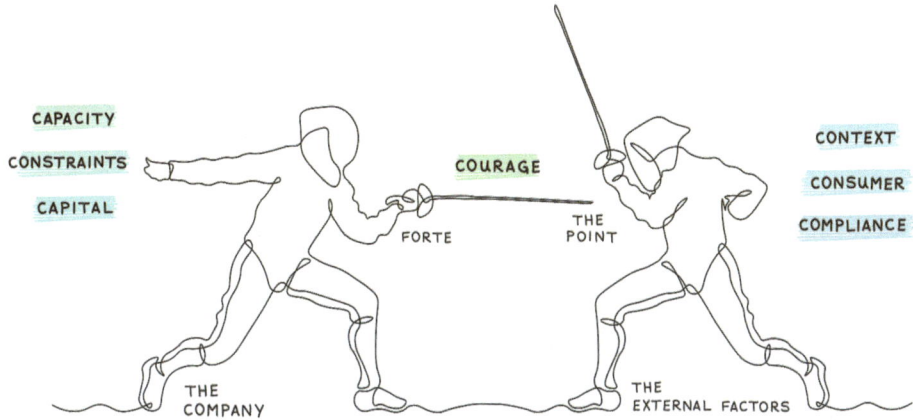

Figure 11-3. *Precision over power. Adapted from Shutterstock*

The importance of precision holds true in business. Every action, decision, and strategy should be pointed at an organization's core purpose: its strategic "point." This ensures that resources are used efficiently, efforts are focused, and the organization acts cohesively toward its objectives. When, instead, an organization makes broad sweeping corrections, it's wasting time, resources, and energy because it isn't concentrated on a single point. In other words, organizations need to align people, processes, and strategies to stay true to their core missions.

The great challenge for any organization lies in maintaining this alignment—ensuring that as the company evolves, grows, and navigates through periods of change, its people and processes remain centered around this core purpose. It's easy to stay aligned for a day. It takes a tremendous amount of effort to stay aligned every day. Keeping everyone headed in the same direction, with a shared understanding of what the company aims to achieve requires maintaining a balance between flexibility and steadfastness, so the organization can make adaptations without losing sight of its foundational purpose.

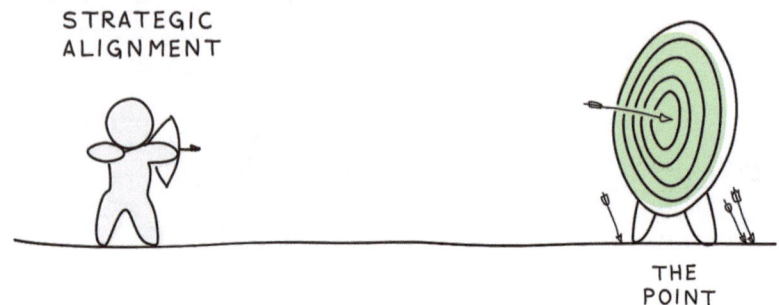

Figure 11-4. Strategic alignment to the point

Focusing on the internal aspects of a business—capacity, constraints, and capital—provides a framing to identify areas for improvement or investment. These three components are deeply interrelated and affect a company's ability to achieve its objectives.

Capacity: Do we have the necessary resources and capacity to deliver on our customer-experience goals?

This includes

- Physical Resources: Machinery, technology, facilities, and raw materials

- Human Resources: Skills, expertise, and the number of employees

- Process Efficiency: The effectiveness of operational processes and workflows

Capacity determines the maximum output a company can achieve under optimal conditions. Increasing capacity can involve investments in scaling existing technology across other parts of the business, hiring additional staff, or improving operational processes.

Constraints: What are our current limitations (e.g., budget, manpower, technology) that could hinder the delivery of exceptional customer experiences?

- Technological Limitations: Outdated systems or equipment that hinder productivity

- Financial Restrictions: Limited funds for investment in growth or improvement initiatives

- Skill Gaps: Lack of necessary expertise or knowledge among the workforce

- Process Inefficiencies: Bottlenecks or redundant processes that waste time and resources

Identifying and addressing constraints is crucial for improving operational efficiency and unlocking growth. Understanding your constraints means you know which blockers are preventing innovation, as well as which of your innovation pathways are technically feasible.

Capital: How much capital is available and how can it be best allocated to overcome constraints and enhance our delivery capabilities?

- Expanding Capacity: Purchasing new equipment or expanding facilities.

- Overcoming Constraints: Investing in technology upgrades, training for employees, or hiring new talent.

- Innovation and Growth: Funding new product development, marketing initiatives, or entering new markets. Capital allocation decisions are strategic, determining which areas of the business receive investment and how these investments are prioritized to support the company's goals.

Relationship Between Capacity, Constraints, and Capital

Capacity and Constraints: Capacity is often limited by internal constraints such as bottlenecks or inefficiencies. Recognizing and addressing constraints can unlock additional capacity without necessarily requiring significant capital investment. For example, streamlining a process may increase output without the need for new machinery.

Constraints and Capital: Financial resources allow a company to overcome constraints directly by investing in solutions like new technologies, employee training, or operational improvements. However, capital itself can be a constraint if financial resources are limited.

Capital and Capacity: Expanding capacity often involves purchasing new equipment, hiring additional staff, or upgrading infrastructure—all of which require capital investment.

Decisions about where to invest capital should consider where increases in capacity will have the most significant impact on the company's ability to meet its goals. Effective management involves understanding these connections and making strategic choices that address the need to expand capacity, overcome constraints, and invest capital wisely. This balance is necessary for sustainable growth and competitiveness.

Key Takeaways

- Visionary leadership, exemplified by innovators like Henry Ford and Steve Jobs, coupled with a design-led approach, is crucial for businesses to achieve disruptive innovation and sustainable transformation in their industries.

- The 7Cs framework (Courage, Capacity, Consumer, Context, Constraints, Capital, and Compliance) outlines essential conditions for organizations, guiding them to not only innovate but disrupt and transform their fields in a financially sustainable manner.

CHAPTER 12

Looking Ahead: Design as a Force for Good

Today, we face unprecedented changes in how we interact with people, products, society, and the environment—forcing us to radically rethink how we operate. Rather than remaining inwardly focused, it's time to drive design's impact outward. Design has the potential to be a powerful catalyst for change. It has the power to extend our influence beyond our organizations and into the communities we serve. This requires designers to adopt new ways of thinking and working to explore design strategies that make a positive impact. By harnessing design as a force for good, we can create meaningful change, address pressing social issues, and build a more equitable and sustainable future.

In this chapter, you will learn

- The next frontier of design impact—"Design as a Force for Good"

- Design's role in sustainable transformation and leading organizational change

Leading Organizational Change Toward Sustainability

Businesses are no longer judged solely on their profitability; they are increasingly held accountable for their impact on the environment, society, and the well-being of individuals and communities. The old paradigm of profit maximization at any cost is being replaced by a new ethos that recognizes the interdependence of business success and societal well-being. The driving force behind this imperative is the pressing need to align with global goals and to create shared value for all stakeholders.

The scale of sustainable transformation required in the coming years will demand a major realignment across industries. Transforming established companies to think sustainably will mean overhauling traditional organizational structures and teams. Design is uniquely positioned to drive this change. Skilled design teams collaborating across functions—with sustainability experts modeling environmental impact, engineers conducting life cycle analyses, supply chain partners instituting circular protocols and finance leaders measuring progress—can together develop the roadmap to a more sustainable future. This will mean letting go of outdated cost-focused thinking and embracing creative ways of delivering products and services in a way that regenerates natural and social systems. This shared value approach is the only way businesses can ensure environmental sustainability and social responsibility over the long term.

Armed with the tools, frameworks, and methodologies discussed in the book, designers can lay the foundation for a broader transformation that sets the stage for a new era of sustainability. It will require a holistic approach that touches every department, team, and process within the organization. It will extend beyond the organization's immediate boundaries, requiring partnerships and alliances with suppliers, customers, regulatory bodies, and communities. Together, these diverse stakeholders can pool their collective expertise, experiences, and perspectives to develop innovative solutions at every point across their value chain.

Design as a Force for Good is the new frontier. This frontier embodies the idea that design, with its capacity for innovation, empathy, and problem-solving, can serve as a powerful catalyst for positive change. It compels organizations to evolve from a narrow focus on internal excellence to a broader commitment to positively addressing global challenges.

Design's Role in Addressing Global Challenges

Why should we as designers embrace "Design as a Force for Good"? As my design colleague so eloquently put it, "sustainability issues are actually UX issues." Design choices have a significant impact not just on end users but also on the environment. Increasingly, we see that these environmental risks have a significant impact on a company's bottom line.

Prior to my career shift into digital, my background was in architecture and the design of real-world spaces. The design choices we made not only impacted the bottom line but also had social and environmental impacts. A choice between whether to put bathtubs or showers in public housing might seem trivial—with the effect on the water bill for you or I being of little concern—but for low-income tenants, it can make a big difference.

ESG (Environmental, Social, Governance) is a framework that helps stakeholders understand how an organization manages risks and opportunities related to environmental, social, and governance criteria—often referred to as ESG factors. It provides a comprehensive lens for evaluating a company's long-term sustainability, recognizing that responsible business practices extend beyond profitability alone. The framework emphasizes the interconnectedness of these three pillars:

environmental impact, social responsibility, and sound governance practices. By taking this holistic view, ESG encourages companies to address a wide range of issues, from reducing carbon emissions and promoting diversity to ensuring ethical governance and transparency. This approach helps businesses create sustainable value, build trust with stakeholders, and remain resilient in a rapidly evolving regulatory landscape.

ESG principles are better observed by some companies than by others. In 2023, ExxonMobil—which according to Yahoo Finance is one of the most hated companies in America—gave money to Baton Rouge's Food Bank.[1,2] Now, I'm not suggesting that Baton Rouge's Food Bank is not a worthy cause but I imagine most of us would prefer to see ExxonMobil take proactive measures to address their own impact on the environment, as well as accountability for its long history of environmental disasters.

Aligning ESG principles to address the external impacts of ExxonMobil's corporate strategy would help to create more meaningful and sustainable change. By prioritizing ESG goals—such as reducing carbon emissions, investing in renewable energy, and promoting ethical governance—ExxonMobil could create shared value. Given that many investment funds now assess the ESG credentials of their investment targets, companies like ExxonMobil can now structure their incentives to align profitability and sustainability.

So how can we align these seemingly conflicting priorities? We can use frameworks like TRACES to realign around this new strategic goal—transforming existing systems and incentive structures to include

---

[1] Haqqi, Ty, "15 Most Hated Companies in America," Yahoo Finance, 25 Dec. 2022, www.finance.yahoo.com/news/15-most-hated-companies-america-230921187.html.

[2] ExxonMobil Pipeline Company, "ExxonMobil Pipeline Company Partners with Greater Baton Rouge Food Bank for Holiday Meal Distribution Events," ExxonMobil Pipeline, 23 Dec. 2023, www.exxonmobilpipeline.com/en/news-and-updates/br-food-distribution.

sustainability considerations. Then we must ensure that our internal stakeholders have a shared understanding around what this change should look like. Importantly, this includes expressing sustainability initiatives in a way that incorporates not only the cost of doing it but also the cost of *not* doing it. This ensures we can balance sustainability and profit using a common currency and that we have the desired impact across the business and its stakeholders. In other words, this is how we can Create Shared Value (CSV).

Creating Shared Value Through Design

Creating Shared Value (CSV) aligns corporate objectives and societal well-being. Instead of viewing these as conflicting goals, CSV demonstrates that business success and societal progress can be mutually reinforcing. What benefits society and the planet also benefits the business's bottom line.

The Triple Bottom Line—people, profit, and planet—emphasizes that organizations should not only be responsible for financial (profit) success but also their social impact (people) as well as their impact on environmental stewardship (planet). The term was introduced by British business consultant and sustainability advocate John Elkington in 1994. Businesses have an opportunity to build trust and relevance by moving from reactive to proactive, from isolated to collaborative. The era of profits-chasing and short-term views must give way to shared values that serve the common good.

Life Centered Design: Disrupting the Evolution of the Design Thinking Industry and Transforming Systems for Good

Maria Edwards is a product and experience leader with 14+ years of B2B and B2C expertise. Maria has scaled digital transformations across diverse industries, including retail, finance, travel, and e-commerce. She is a fractional design leader, coaching business startups across innovation through HCD, circular design across sustainability, and CX strategies across regional and global outreach programs.

In this era of rapid technological advancement, especially with the rise of new technologies such as AI, we have an unprecedented opportunity to shape industries ethically with a focus on environmental and social responsibility. This requires shifting our design focus beyond human-centeredness to life-centered design. By considering the impact our creations have on all living beings and the planet, we can begin to design solutions that contribute to a regenerative future.

Circular design, which prioritizes minimizing waste and maximizing resource reuse, is a powerful tool for aligning design strategy with sustainability goals. Incorporating circular design, with speculative futures design, especially as it has abilities to envision multiple futures, can enable solutions to drive disruptive transformation. As an example, many FMCG and retail companies have phased out single-use plastics.I

(continued)

Life Centered Design: Disrupting the Evolution of the Design Thinking Industry and Transforming Systems for Good

In the regulated FMCG and retail industry, the transition away from single-use plastics is a prime example of where circular design and speculative futures thinking has driven meaningful change. We worked within a complex system of government, packaging manufacturers, retailers, and consumers united with a disruptive vision aligning with our overall ESG strategic values, to ban non-compostable, single-use plastic bags across Australia. This involved collaborating closely with a nationaretailer and a strong cross-functional taskforce to realize our ambition. Leveraging the methods of speculative and circular design, you can unlock opportunities, steering solutions with infinite possible futures, and identify risks associated with such a highly complex transformation.

Well-conceived business strategies, supported with the outputs created to craft new experiences such as service blueprints and new circular flows, enable teams to envision feasible changes throughout the ecosystem. Teams can visualize changes more readily and comprehend the vast breadth of underlying impacts. An example was defining how we would consider the process in the experience value chain and delivering orders with the selection of new packaging. We considered all underlying impacts centered around the manufacturing process to ensure the packaging complied with the new regulations, through to the information presented to educate customers about the material and manufacturing process used to create the reusable bags.

When embedded through the project, we began to rethink beyond and consider how circular design can lead to innovative packaging solutions, such as

- Reusable containers that consumers return for refills
- Biodegradable or compostable packaging materials that break down naturally
- Packaging designed for disassembly and easy recycling

Redesigning Production Processes: Circularity can be incorporated into manufacturing by

- Using recycled content in new packaging
- Optimizing production processes to minimize waste generation
- Designing products for longevity and easy repair

(*continued*)

Life Centered Design: Disrupting the Evolution of the Design Thinking Industry and Transforming Systems for Good

Engaging Consumers: Circular design thinking extends to consumer behavior:

- Educating consumers about the benefits of circularity and how to participate
- Incentivizing the return of packaging for reuse or recycling
- Creating products that are easy to repair or upgrade, extending their lifespan

By applying circular design principles to the single-use plastics challenge, we delivered on key ESG principles and values that

- Reduce Environmental Impact: Minimizing waste and resource consumption significantly lowers the environmental footprint of products.
- Create New Business Opportunities: Circular models can open new revenue streams, such as refill services or product-as-a-service offerings.

- Enhance Brand Reputation: Demonstrating a commitment to sustainability can strengthen consumer loyalty and brand value.

Success and failure in ESG efforts, as well as the adoption of more social and environmental responsibilities by businesses, industries, and governments, will continue to rely on committed leaders at every organization to drive change and adapt. Once we move through these initial constraints and forge forward, we will find new innovative experiences that serve the generations to come.

—Maria Edwards

Conclusion

The tools presented in this book are united by a common theme: alignment. From the tools we select to the capabilities we build, the customers we serve and the employees we support, every aspect of the organization must connect with our core purpose.

We have an unprecedented opportunity to use design in service of something greater. Once we have aligned our values, capabilities, and goals, we can more effectively tackle the wicked problems that we face. As we look toward the future, design can play a transformative role.

The fundamental question we should ask ourselves is: How can we leave the world a better place? While the question itself seems simple, finding the answer is far more complex. It's not necessarily giving the user what they want—"faster horses," to quote Henry Ford. It's about assessing all angles of our design and how it will be used to channel the desired behaviors in the user. For example, we can design an application for a new form of exchange using blockchain but if the negative (the energy consumption) outweighs the positive (the convenience and democratization) of the application, then can we say it's for the greater good?

We need to broaden our definition of design—not just focusing on how our designs will be used but on the impact of our designs. By doing so, we can truly position design as a "force for good." When we do that, we can break away from the mindset that environmental, social, and governance ESG considerations are inconvenient afterthoughts, and instead integrate them into the core of our design ethos.

Of course, there will always be debates and discussions on what exactly a "force for good" entails. Each person will have a slightly different answer. There will always be room for improvement—designing more efficiently or solving problems faster. Does that mean that taking one step back to take two steps forward is progress? The only way we can answer these questions is through collaborative dialogue and ongoing discussions.

By answering these questions, we redefine how we think of ourselves and our role within the organization and the wider world. When our values, capabilities, and goals align, it creates a powerful synergy, building a united front where each stakeholder feels supported and understood.

This means that every decision, every action, and every strategy taken is filtered through the lens of our core purpose, ensuring that our organizational goals are not disjointed efforts but parts of a cohesive whole. By aligning our tools, capabilities, and people with our purpose, we create an environment where innovation is not just sporadic and random, but a consistent, driven force.

Design *equals* change—it's the process of moving from our current state to a desired future state. When designers and companies align around the concept of Design as a Force for Good, our work and our efforts can contribute to broader sustainability initiatives like the SDGs and the circular economy. Through this shared commitment to design as a catalyst for change, we can cultivate a culture of collaboration that addresses today's challenges while preparing us for the wicked problems that society will face at the furthest frontiers of technology.

Index

© Garkay Wong 2025
G. Wong, *The Art of Design Strategy*, Design Thinking,
https://doi.org/10.1007/979-8-8688-0552-3